The Robertson Family

Portrait of a Post-Civil War African-American Family

"Challenges and Vision"
1860's – Present

EVELYN C. ROBERTSON JR.

authorHOUSE

AuthorHouse™
1663 Liberty Drive
Bloomington, IN 47403
www.authorhouse.com
Phone: 833-262-8899

This book is a work of non-fiction. Unless otherwise noted, the author and the publisher
make no explicit guarantees as to the accuracy of the information contained in this book
and in some cases, names of people and places have been altered to protect their privacy.

Published by AuthorHouse 12/16/2020

ISBN: 978-1-6655-1056-1 (sc)
ISBN: 978-1-6655-1055-4 (hc)
ISBN: 978-1-6655-1054-7 (e)

Library of Congress Control Number: 2020924611

Print information available on the last page.

Any people depicted in stock imagery provided by Getty Images are models,
and such images are being used for illustrative purposes only.
Certain stock imagery © Getty Images.

This book is printed on acid-free paper.

Because of the dynamic nature of the Internet, any web addresses or links contained in
this book may have changed since publication and may no longer be valid. The views
expressed in this work are solely those of the author and do not necessarily reflect the
views of the publisher, and the publisher hereby disclaims any responsibility for them.

Scripture quotations marked HCSB are from the Holman Christian Standard
Bible®. HCSB®. Copyright ©1999, 2000, 2002, 2003 by Holman Bible Publishers.
Used by permission. Holman Christian Standard Bible®, Holman CSB®, and
HCSB® are federally registered trademarks of Holman Bible Publishers

This book is dedicated to and is a tribute to Robertson's past and present for their trials, sacrifices, and struggles known and unknown, the challenges conquered, and opportunities taken. "To God Be the Glory." I dedicate this book to:

My grandfather and grandmother, Crawford Dewitt Robertson and Cora P. Robertson, for their motivation, vision, determination, grit, and hard work. Their focus on self-determination is commendable and awe-inspiring, a model for their generation and generations that followed. Without Crawford and Cora this book would not be possible.

My father and mother, Evelyn C. Robertson Sr. and Pearl B. Robertson, whose love and nurturing made it possible for me and my two brothers to dream, aspire, and become productive citizens and attain success in our chosen endeavors.

To my aunt Myrtle Louise Robertson whose love, sacrifice, support, encouragement, and guidance played an indelible role in helping me navigate the course of life. Without her support this story might have taken a different trajectory.

To my children, Jeffrey and Sheila, and my grandchildren, Malik and Jasmine, always remember that you can achieve anything that you set your heart and mind to.

Acknowledgments

I would like to thank my wife, Hugholene, for her patience and support in my endeavors to complete this project and her untiring support in our many endeavors throughout our fifty-seven-year journey of marriage.

My daughter, Sheila, for her technical support and assistance with this project. I would also like to thank my other relatives that I approached for bits of information about our family.

I want to also thank my friend and classmate Odell Greene for his photographic support for this project.

Contents

Preface

Over the course of the past several years quite a few people have asked me when was I going to write my memoir. I never gave this much thought until recently because I have been more focused on the Robertson family history than any personal achievements that may have come my way. After some insistence, it occurred that maybe this is the time to combine both.

As I have aged, I have become more reflective, which I suppose is a natural phenomenon associated with aging. However, I am still looking forward with faith, hope, and anticipation.

I have been very fortunate and blessed to be able to serve in several high-profile roles, and there may be a natural inquisitiveness about my story. During this era, I had opportunities that were unusual for African Americans from the Deep South. I clearly recognize that I have no story without my family. Any success that I have had is inextricably intertwined with my family. I also recognize that young people and children unborn need to know the story of a family that emanated from humble beginnings dating back before the Civil War. I know that without God this story would not be possible.

I hope that readers will be inspired and a spark created as to possibilities, with the understanding with Faith in God, preparation, hard work, determination and perseverance much can be achieved.

As I began this research, I was amazed with the early Hardeman County leaders and institutional associations and relationships with the Robertson family. Some may be vicarious and possibly by happenstance but still significant to me. I will discuss some of these in detail as I focus on my career and achievements.

Attempting to chronicle the history of a family is no easy task. From my early adult life, I had an innate inquisitiveness about my family and its early origins and how it came to be. I must say there are still many blanks that I have still not filled.

I had the fortune of knowing both of my grandparents on my mother's side of the family, Nat and Mattie Robinson Brewer. Nat was born in 1870 and died in 1957, and Mattie was born in 1876 and died in 1962. My mother, Pearl Brewer Robertson, grew up in Bolivar, Tennessee. She was born on May 7, 1912, and passed on April 13, 1999.

On my father's side of the family, I had the fortune of knowing my grandmother, Cora Pierce Robertson. She was born September 12, 1870, and passed in 1950. My grandfather, Crawford Robertson, was born April 4, 1856, and passed on December 17, 1937. My father, Evelyn C. Robertson Sr., was born July 14, 1909. He was the victim of a homicide on July 16, 1955. At that time, I was fourteen years old and about to enter the ninth grade.

I am very proud of my Brewer heritage, which I have surveyed briefly in an appendix to this present volume.

This book is not a high-five moment about the Robertson family. It is an attempt to provide a humble portrait of an African American Southern family and its survival through the maze called life in uncertain times. It is an attempt to show that resilience, perseverance, strength, and courage have their rewards. It is also an attempt to encourage my children and to motivate my grandchildren and generations to come that the seemingly impossible is possible. I hope that this book can be an inspiration to others regardless of race, color, or national origin.

Introduction

For the purposes of this presentation, I have chosen to focus on the dominant impact of Crawford Robertson, patriarch of the Robertson family, because of the challenges of the times, his legacy, and his reach, even until this day. Having been born on November 19, 1941, I did not have the privilege or the honor of knowing my grandfather. He died in 1937. I do recognize that I stand on his shoulders. Having grown up listening to family and others talk about Crawford Robertson provided great inspiration. His impact along with my grandmother, Cora, provided inspiration and motivation for their six children and propelled each of them to aspire to be the best that they could be.

For an African American family in the middle and late 1800s, life carried with it many challenges. Survival was a real test, and attaining dignity was even more fleeting.

Whiteville, Hardeman County, Tennessee, is located approximately sixty miles from the so-called Fort Pillow Massacre that occurred in 1864, in which a garrison of nearly six hundred soldiers, half of whom were black, were slaughtered. Whiteville is also located 135 miles from Pulaski, Tennessee, where the Ku Klux Klan was founded. Between 1866 and 1869, the Klan systematically perpetrated terror and violence on blacks throughout Tennessee. Unfortunately, this was the societal atmosphere in which African Americans lived at this time. Whiteville and Hardeman County were no exception.

Born into slavery in 1856, Crawford achieved the remarkable feat of navigating the maze of slavery and the travails of the Civil War. He was emancipated at nine years old. Crawford's mother, Cornelia Robertson, was born in 1833 in Virginia. She is interred in the Union Hill Cemetery in Whiteville, Tennessee. Crawford's siblings included Monterey, born in 1850; Harriett, born in 1853; Cora, born in 1857; Howell, born in 1860; and Maggie, born in 1860. There will be more about Maggie later. A sister, Babe, was born in 1866. Henry Neely in some records is listed as Crawford's father; however, based on census information, this is questionable since Crawford is variously listed as mulatto, along with several of his siblings.

The ship that brought Crawford's ancestors to these shores and the date are unknown. I don't even know who enslaved his family. I do know that this family has a mixture of several ethnic identities, as attested in my own DNA, which will be referred to later in this research. Though the unknowns are perplexing, this is reality for most African American families. The key is to accept it and move forward. I hope that this research demonstrates that that is what the Robertson's have attempted to do.

Imagining life for Crawford as an ex-slave across the gulf of two generations is difficult. I do know that it took courage, fortitude, and fate to pursue the path that he took that has now manifested itself as this Robertson family. As imperfect as we are, we still stand. I submit that we are standing on the promises as penned by R. Kelso Carter in his song, "Standing on the Promises." One stanza says,

> Standing on the promises that cannot fail,
> When the howling storms of doubt and fear assail,
> By the living word of God I shall prevail,
> Standing on the promises of God.

I know that God's mighty hand has been on this family.

No family is perfect, and circumstances and challenges are ever present. Still, the resilience of this family and its success is a story that should be told. Certainly, there are many other examples of this resilience and strength by African American families, many in our small community. I commend them and encourage their continued resilience and admonish them to stay strong and tell their own stories.

The historic struggle of the African American family, its relevance and its structure are real and we must be vigilant to preserve it. The family fabric must remain strong; our survival is dependent on it. If we cannot pass this test, the struggle, the humiliation, the degradation of our ancestors will be for naught, and we certainly cannot allow that to occur. With some of the progress that our society has made, I still find myself perplexed by some of the present conditions and circumstances of our modern-day families; we must learn from the past.

I

Hardeman County, Tennessee

IT IS IMPOSSIBLE TO PROVIDE this portrait of the Robertson family without first describing the early history of Hardeman County. Its location, geography, and people are all relevant to the story that needs to be told.

The county lies in the upper plateau of West Tennessee near the headwaters of the Big Hatchie River. The Big Hatchie is the principal drainage of the county. Its tributaries are Little Hatchie, Wade Creek, Piney Creek, Gray Creek, Mill Creek, Clever Creek, Hickory Creek, Clear Creek, Pleasant Run, Spring Creek, Cub Creek, Porter Creek, Muddy Creek, and numerous smaller streams. The water in these streams is comparatively clear. Good drinking water is easily found by digging or boring. The soil is well adapted for the growth of cotton and the cereals. Garden products are mainly potatoes, beans, and peas. The dairy products are also valuable. An increase in pasturelands and a more extensive growth of grasses brings about very profitable stock raising. The Illinois Central and the Memphis & Charleston railroads afforded ample facilities for market, while the Hatchie and its tributaries afforded good facilities for mills, gins, and other machinery. Some very valuable timbers are found in Hardeman County.

The treaty that opened western Tennessee for settlement by the whites was signed on October 19, 1818, by Isaac Shelby and Andrew Jackson for President Monroe and the chiefs and leading men for the Chickasaw Indians. The territory was allowed to the Indians as hunting ground for two years longer, so that it was not until about 1820 that the whites were given an opportunity to settle within the territory. The rapid progress of settlement is seen from the fact that the courts were organized in the fall of 1823, and the census of 1830 shows a population of 11,655, half of that shown on the 1880 census. The rapid settlement came in from North and South Carolina, Virginia, northern Alabama, and middle Tennessee.

The first to enter this county for permanent residence came in 1819 and 1820. Col. Thomas J. Hardeman, for whom the county was named, became the first county clerk. Also Col. Ezekiel Polk immigrated with his son William Polk and son-in-law Thomas McNeal. William Polk was the first chairman of the county court. Thomas McNeal was the father of the prominent McNeal family of Bolivar.

Hardeman County is one of the middle tier counties of west Tennessee. It is bounded on the north by Haywood and Madison Counties; on the east by Chester and McNairy Counties; on the south by the State of Mississippi; and on the west by Fayette and Haywood Counties.

The first railroad in the county was the Memphis & Charleston. This was chartered February 4, 1846, with a capital stock of $800,000.

Steps were taken by the General Assembly of 1884–85 for the erection of the third asylum for the unfortunate of the state, and $85,000 was appropriated as a nucleus of the amount for the new institution. In the summer of 1886, a site for the asylum was selected lying two and one-half miles west of Bolivar. One hundred acres out of a 738-acre tract was purchased by the commissioners, Dr. W. P. Jones, Dr. J. H. Callender, and Hon. John M. East, from Paul T. Jones, et al., for $80,000, with the refusal of any or all of the remainder at $20 per acre. The asylum, as it was known originally, is now Western Mental Health Institute.

The principal businesses of Bolivar were the following firms:

- General stores – Kahn Bros., D. E. Durrett, J. A. Wilson & Son, and Barrett and Bro.;
- Groceries – G. T. Ferguson, Joseph Tate, W. A. Mercer, Jones Bros., W. H. Reynolds, and W. J. Redd;
- Drugstores – Emerson & Savage and B. V. Hudson; and
- Liverymen – Emerson & Savage, Noah Nuckolls, and Nooner & Newbern.

The hotels are the Houston House and Acton House. The first newspaper published in the place was the *Bolivar Palladium*, published some time before 1830. Then followed the *Bolivar Herald* and then the *Bolivar Democrat*, which was founded about 1845 by J. J. Neely and continued to the war. The *Bolivar Bulletin* was founded in 1866 by M. R. Parrish.

The bank at Bolivar, the first in the history of the town, was chartered in September 1866 by W. C. Dorion, G. T. Ingram, Isaac Kahn, C. A. Miller, W. A. Mercer, W. T. Anderson, A. T. McNeal, D. E. Durrett, J. Norment, R. M. Wright, J. C. Savage, and W. Durden. The capital stock was $30,000. The officers were A. T. McNeal, president; and W. C. Dorion, cashier. The directors were A. T. McNeal, D. E. Durrett, W. A. Mercer. W. C. Dorion, Sam'l Kahn, Austin Miller, and G. T. Ingram.

Isaac and Samuel Kahn, under the firm title of Kahn Bros., were leading dry good merchants of Bolivar. They were the sons of Henry and Louise (Newberger) Kahn, both natives of Germany, where they grew up and were married. Soon after, they immigrated to America and located in Bolivar, where he opened a dry goods store and engaged in this business until 1863. He then moved to Louisville, Kentucky, where he carried on the same business a short time and retired in 1868. He died in 1880.

They had five children—four sons and one daughter. In 1868 the four sons came to Bolivar and opened a large dry goods house, running it in partnership for fifteen years. In 1883 Marcus Kahn left the firm and a year later Jacob Kahn withdrew. Twice the store was burned, and each time a more extensive one was built.

Isaac, the senior member of the firm, was born July 20, 1849, in Bolivar, where he received his early education and afterward attended the Male High School at Louisville, Kentucky. After completing his education, he came to Bolivar and engaged in the family business. In 1880 he married Emma Rosenthal, by whom he had two sons, Henry and Claude Mellville. Samuel, the junior member of the firm, was born in 1852 in Bolivar and received the same educational advantages as his brother Isaac. In 1881 he married Tillie Frank, and to this union three children were born: Annie, Louise, and an infant. The firm of Kahn Bros. were the leading dry goods business in Bolivar from 1868 and were prominent among first businesses in the town.

Whiteville, Tennessee, is my hometown, as Robertsons have lived here since the early to mid-1880s. It is surrounded by some of the best farming land in the county. Whiteville was among the earliest settled communities in Hardeman County.

Among the earlier inhabitants of the place were T. B. Norment, C. W. Henry, J. S. Buford, G. Davis, B. A. Henry, D. Caldwell, J. S. Osborne, J. C. Parner, Orin Harris, W. W. Farley, B. A. Harris, John Warner, J. S. Bayley, T. N. Brown, C. H. Williams, G. A. Sanders, J. C. Green, and J. S. Norment. The place was incorporated in October 1854.

Dr. John S. Robertson, a farmer and retired physician of Whiteville, was born July 7, 1819, in Wake County, North Carolina, the only surviving member of a family of nine children born to John and Mary (Barrham) Robertson. The father was a native of the same state and county as his son. The mother was born in Virginia but immigrated with her parents when a small child to North Carolina, where she was married. Both were of Scotch-Irish extraction. In 1820 they moved to Madison County, Tennessee, being among the first settlers west of the Tennessee River. They were not connected with any church but were honorable and respected people. The father was a Whig, a planter throughout his life and very prosperous. He employed a large number of hands. His death occurred in 1821, after which the mother lived with the family until 1852, when she departed this life.

About the time that John S. attained his majority, he began the study of medicine; he later took a course in Ohio Eclectic Medical School at Cincinnati, where he graduated in 1844. He immediately began to practice in Henderson County and in 1848 located in Hardeman County, three miles west of Whiteville, where he exercised his profession as well as agriculture, meeting with success in both. In 1870 he moved into the town.

For fifteen years he was postmaster, at the same time keeping a drug store. After thirty-four years of active and profitable practice he retired from his professional duties in 1880 and turned his attention to his plantation. He owned 700 acres of valuable land. In 1844 the doctor married Miss Amanda M. Wood, born in Henderson County, October 1, 1826. To their union three sons and one daughter were born: Andrew L., who was in the army under Gen. Forrest's command and was killed at the battle of Memphis; Eugenia C.; Christopher W., also in Forrest's command; and John B. Mrs. Robertson was a true Christian woman, an earnest member of the Methodist church. Her death occurred in 1860.

Three years later the doctor wedded Miss Nannie M. Carnes, who was born April 4, 1835. This marriage resulted in the birth of two children: Mary W. and Carnes. Dr. and Mrs. Robertson were active and esteemed members of the Methodist church.[1]

Western Mental Health Institute,

Hardeman County Courthouse,

---

[1] Goodspeed Histories – Hardeman & Fayette County, pages 818–819, 822, 827–828, 831, 921–922, 947–948.

Interior Marker of Courthouse, circa 1992.

II

Struggle for Identity after the Civil War

"**L**IFT EVERY VOICE AND SING," a song most African Americans know from school or church and often referred to as the black national anthem, depicts the struggle for identity after the Civil War and even the African American search for identity today. Dr. Shana Redmond, a professor at UCLA who studies music, race, and politics and author of the book *Anthem: Social Movements and the Sound of Solidarity in the African Diaspora*, says it's a song about transcending difficulties, and those difficulties have never fully receded.

The first verse opens with a command to optimism, praise, and freedom. The second verse reminds us to never forget the suffering and obstacles of the past. The third and final stanza is about the challenges of the future. They are to be met with perseverance, courage, faith, and trust in God.

"Lift every Voice and Sing" was written at a pivotal time, when Jim Crow was replacing slavery and African Americans were searching for an identity. Author and activist James Weldon Johnson wrote the words as a poem, which his brother John set to music. James Weldon Johnson once was associated with Fisk University, which is referred to later in this research. This song spoke to the history of the dark journey of African Americans, says current NAACP president Derrick Johnson and for that matter many Africans in the diaspora who struggled to get a place of hope.[2]

---

[2] Article, Till Victory Is Won: The Staying Power of Lift Every Voice and Sing; NPR- https://www.npr.org/ 2018/08/1616383249201American-Anthem-Lift Every Voice-And Sing-Black National Anthem.

Crawford Robertson was born into slavery and at the end of the Civil War was nine years old. Following the Civil War there were many questions. Who was an American? What rights should all Americans enjoy? Were former slaves American citizens? When and how would former confederates regain their citizenship? What form of labor would replace slavery?

Black Southern Americans, even though free, lived in desperate rural poverty. Having been denied education and wages under slavery, ex-slaves were often forced by necessity of their economic circumstances to rent land from their white slave owners. These sharecroppers paid rent on the land by giving a portion of their crop to the landowner.

In a few places in the South, former slaves seized land from former owners in the immediate aftermath of the Civil War. However, federal troops quickly restored the land to the white landowners.

For African Americans in the South, life after slavery was a world transformed. Gone were the brutalities and indignities of slave life, the whippings and sexual assaults, the selling and forcible relocations of family members, the denial of education, wages, etc.

After slavery, governments across the South instituted laws known as black codes. These laws granted certain legal rights to blacks, including the right to marry, own property, and sue in court, but the codes also made it illegal for blacks to serve on juries, testify against whites, or serve in the state militias. The black codes also required black sharecroppers and tenant farmers to sign annual labor contracts with white landowners. If they refused, they could be arrested and hired out for work.

During the period of Reconstruction, which lasted from 1865 to 1877, Congress passed and enforced laws that promoted civil and political rights for African Americans across the South. Most notable among these laws were three amendments to the US Constitution: the Thirteenth Amendment (1865) ended slavery, the Fourteenth Amendment (1868) guaranteed African Americans the rights of American citizenship, and the Fifteenth Amendment (1870) guaranteed blacks the right to vote.

In 1870, only approximately 30,000 African Americans in the South owned land, usually small plots. This compared with four million others.

The end of the Civil War and the Reconstruction of the South attempted to address some of the social concerns of the freed slaves but in reality could do very little to make blacks economically and politically equal to whites.

That African Americans became American citizens was arguably the signal development during Reconstruction. Only a decade earlier the Supreme Court had ruled in the Dred Scott decision in 1858 that people of African descent imported into the United States and held as slaves could never be citizens of the United States.

The emotional burden of relief from the aftermath of the Civil War was somewhat alleviated by the emergence of the black Methodist and Baptist churches. Through their evangelical roots, they used spiritual song and gospel; they were the forerunner of Southern Baptist Churches. The African Methodist Episcopal (AME) church sent missionaries to the South immediately after the Civil War.

Family, church, and school became centers of black life after slavery. Black churches became centerpieces of African American culture and community, not only as places of personal spiritual renewal and communal worship but also centers for learning, socializing, and political organization. Black ministers were community leaders.

African Americans' desire for education found expression in the establishment of schools at every level, from basic education to the founding of the nation's first black colleges such as Fisk and Howard University. Allen-White School in Whiteville, Tennessee, is an example of this desire at the secondary school level. Additional commentary about its role will be discussed later.

To help blacks reenter society, the Freedmen's Bureau was created as part of the Reconstruction Act. It was a federal agency designed to provide food, clothes, and shelter for freed slaves and whites in need. White and black teachers came south and began to teach the freed slaves. Booker T. Washington said, "It was a whole race going to school. Few were too young and none were too old."

Reconstruction was not very successful in creating real economic freedom. Many called sharecropping and tenant farming economic slavery because it still kept freedmen subservient to whites and at their whim.[3]

---

[3] Article, Khan Academy, Life After Slavery for African Americans, pages 1–7. https://www.khanacademy.org/humanities/us-history/civil-war-era/reconstruction/a/life-after-slavery

The early life of Crawford Robertson was obviously fraught with the conditions previously described and his family was clearly in the sharecropping model of the period following the Civil War. With the lack of education and the implementation of the black codes, his early life had to be very challenging. Little is known about his youth and early adult life. Whose farm did his family live on? What laborious tasks and indignities did his family endure? As a mulatto was he afforded any favor? What sparked his interest and desire to be a landowner himself? These are questions that have perplexed me.

I have often wished that I had been more inquisitive when my relatives closer to Crawford's generation—my father, aunts and uncles, and others—might have provided some insight. I hope and trust that at some point answers to these questions will be found. It is clear that through Crawford's early experiences he was motivated to pursue his own destiny and not accept life of subservience. It is clear not only that his will was evident but also that he had tremendous support in his endeavors. Perhaps his Caucasian relatives played a role in aiding and supporting him.

Living under formidable odds, Crawford Robertson labored in an environment that may have unwittingly contributed to his desire to aspire, desire, dream, and pursue self-determination. His will to work hard and to make sacrifices to make his dream a reality is very evident.

Though there are gaps between Crawford's early life and his early adult life it is apparent that he connected with community individuals that potentially could help aid him to realize his dream. At several points this is evident. Once opportunities arose, he used these relationships to benefit not only his family but others as well. Known then as a second-class citizen, Crawford displayed characteristics and traits that were admirable and were respected by those he encountered. His focus on being a good citizen and raising a respectable family, with a focus on education for his children, has paid dividends even to this date. Putting God first was a trait that aided Crawford in his journey through life. His work ethic, honesty, integrity, perseverance, and creativity were traits that he embodied. He obviously understood how important it was in 1886 to save his money to fuel his dream. This permitted him to purchase land,

and he continued to purchase until 1904, amassing nearly 200 acres which remains in the family 134 years later.

James Baldwin once said, "If you know from where you came, there are no limits as to where you can go". I believe that Crawford knew from whence he came.

III

Patriarch – Crawford Robertson

A good name is better than fine perfume and the day
of one's death than the day of one's birth.
—Ecclesiastes 7:1

Family Tree

CORNELIA ROBERTSON, MOTHER OF CRAWFORD Robertson was born in 1833 in Botetourt, Virginia. In the 1850 US Federal Census, she was listed as fifteen years of age. Her household members were Matthew Robertson, 46; Mary Robertson, 50; John W. Robertson, 22; Cornelia Robertson, 15; Chastaine Robertson, 13; and Sara J. Robertson, 7.

In the 1870 census, Crawford Robertson was listed as born in 1856 and was fourteen years old in 1870. At the end of the Civil War he was nine years old. The household members during this census period were Cornelia, 38; Monterey, 20 (born in 1850); Harriet, 17, (b. 1853); Cora, 13 (b. 1857); Howell, 10 (b. 1860); Babe, 4 (b. 1866); and Elnora, born 1868. According to the census, all of the above were listed as mulatto.

Henry Neely born in 1825 is listed as father of Maggie Neely, who was born in 1860. Maggie Neely is the half-sister of Crawford Robertson.

(See Generation and Descendant Charts)

On September 22, 1877, at age twenty-one, Crawford Robertson married Hannah Waddel. Hannah was twenty-seven. To this union two children were born, Dewitt and Ada. Little is known about Dewitt and Ada. Little was said about these children in my presence as a child or even after I became an adult. My Aunt Myrtle did acknowledge that these children did exist.

In some early census reports they were a part of the Robertson household. In the 1900 census, Ada was listed as fourteen years old and Dewitt was listed as twelve years old. In the 1900 census they resided in Cora and Crawford Robertson's household. Crawford and Cora are my grandparents. What happened to Hannah Waddell? When and where did she die? As for Ada and Dewitt, there is evidence that they later resided on Institute Street in Jackson, Tennessee.

On September 12, 1892 Crawford married Cora Pierce in Fayette County, Tennessee. Her parents were Andy and Ann Pierce. In the 1870 census Cora was listed as one year old. In the 1880 Census she was listed as eleven years of age, and her parents, Andy and Ann, were listed as twenty-seven and twenty-five, respectively.

The union of Crawford and Cora produced seven children: Guy, Johnnie, Vivian, Eleanor, Myrtle and Evelyn. One child, named Little Crawford, died as an infant.

Evelyn C. Robertson Jr.

DESCENDANT CHART

MATTHEW ROBERTSON ------------------------ MARY

[JOHN W] ------------------------------- [CORNELIA]
[CHASTAINE] ----------------------------- [SARAH]

[CORNELIA] 1830-1908 ----------------------- [-HENRY NEELY] 1823 –

** [MONTEREY] 1850 - 1885   ** [HARRIET] 1853 -

* [CRAWFORD 1856-1937]   ** [CORA] 1857- 1923

** [HOWELL] 1860-   ** [MAGGIE] 1860-1947

** [BABE] 1866 -   ** [ELNORA 1868 –

• GRANDFATHER
** GREAT AUNTS & UNCLES

GENERATION 4

MY PARENTS –

EVELYN SR. & PEARL

MY UNCLES & AUNTS & SPOUSES
GUY & NEILA
VIVIAN & DORA
ELEANOR PEARL & BOB BEARD
JOHNNY –
MYRTLE –

GENERATION 5

Evelyn, Brothers & COUSINS –
EVELYN JR. & HUGHOLENE
Darnell & Margaret James & Patricia

ELVESTA & ANN
GUY JR. & LOUISE
CLAUDE & RUTH
PEARL & HERMAN
VIVIAN JR. & CATHY

FAMILY TREE

GREAT GRANDMOTHER

{Cornelia}   1830-1908
   |
CHILDREN
   |
Monterey   1850 - 1885
   |
Harriet   1853 -
   |
Crawford   1856-1937
   |
Cora   1857 - 1923
   |
Howell   1860 -
   |
Maggie   1860-1947
   |
Babe   1866 -
   |
Elnora   1868 -

FAMILY CHART

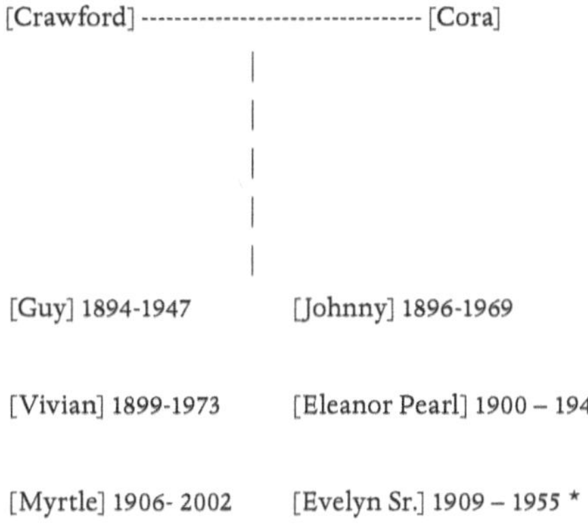

[Crawford] ---------------------------------- [Cora]

[Guy] 1894-1947   [Johnny] 1896-1969

[Vivian] 1899-1973   [Eleanor Pearl] 1900 – 1943

[Myrtle] 1906- 2002   [Evelyn Sr.] 1909 – 1955 *

*   My Father

Known spouses of Crawford's brothers and sisters include Monterey, who married Rosetta Dickinson; Cora in 1876 married Granville Norment; Howell in 1882 married Mollie Hudson and later in 1893 Emma Robertson; and Maggie in 1896 married John Bills. Other sibling relationships are not known to the author.

Father, Evelyn Robertson Sr.,

Mother Pearl Robertson

IV

The Quest and Desire for Land Ownership

THE ROBERTSON FAMILY FARM WAS bought in three tracts beginning in 1888. The properties are recorded in the following deed books:

- Deed Book GG Page 340, December 18, 1888 – 75 Acres,
- Deed Book KK Page 178, January 25, 1896 – 12 Acres, and
- Deed Book PP Page 119, January 25, 1904 – 100.5 acres.

All of these properties are currently owned by Crawford Robertson's grandson, Evelyn C. Robertson Jr. and wife Hugholene. Deeds are recorded at the Hardeman County Court House in Bolivar, Tennessee.

It is important to point out here that even though the original tract of land was deeded on December 18, 1888, a down payment on this tract was made in November 1886 in the amount of $200. The total purchase for the original tract was $562. Excluding down payment, the purchase plan was $181 per annum at a 6 percent interest rate. The seller was W. E. Farley and his wife Susana E. Farley. In 1886, $562 was equivalent in purchasing power of $15,465 in 2020.

Who was W. E. Farley? William E. Farley was a white male born around 1854 who lived in Whiteville, Tennessee. In the 1910 census he and his family lived on Woodlawn Avenue in Whiteville. In 1910 he had been married to his wife Susanna for thirty-three years. His occupation was listed as traveling salesman. He was also involved in the wholesale dry goods business and was also a merchant. Household occupants based on the 1910 census included William E. Farley, 56; Susanna Farley, 50; Edora Farley, 24; Janie P. Farley, 22; Myron Farley, 10; and Subon Davids, 2.

The obvious question is What was the relationship between Crawford and William Farley? It is clear that this opportunity created other opportunities for land ownership. Mr. Farley died on August 15, 1932.

The second tract of land was purchased from S. L. Vaught and wife Martha Vaught in 1896. Mr. Vaught was born in 1816 and died in 1897. The land associated with this purchase was twelve acres. Mr. Vaught was a white male and was born in Tennessee. He was a farmer by occupation. His wife Martha was forty-four years old in the 1860 census. Mr. Vaught was also forty-four years old when this census was conducted. The cost associated with this purchase was $132.

The third tract of land was purchased from Isaac Kahn and wife Emma. This purchase was for 100.5 acres and was made in 1904. The purchase price was $700. Isaac and Samuel Kahn, under the firm title of Kahn Bros., were leading dry goods merchants of Bolivar and the sons of Henry and Louise (Newberger) Kahn, both natives of Germany where they grew up and were married. Isaac was born July 20, 1849, in Bolivar, Tennessee, where he received his early education and afterward attended the Male High School in Louisville, Kentucky. After completing his education, he came to Bolivar. In 1880 he married Emma Rosenthal, by whom he had two sons: Henry and Claude Mellville. The Kahn brothers had the leading dry goods business in Bolivar and were prominent among the first businessmen of the town.[4]

The relationships between Crawford Robertson and the sellers of these properties are obviously questions that the writer has pondered for many years. For the original purchase in 1886 to have been maintained for now 134 years is a feat that Crawford likely could not have imagined. It is clear that not only fate but God's hand has been on this family through many generations, and we are grateful. I am a third generation Robertson to be associated with this farm. The farm was the primary source of income and livelihood for generations. To have the foresight and vision to own land and be self-sufficient as an African American in the late 1800s following a divisive Civil War, Reconstruction, and the Jim

---

[4] *Hardeman County Journal* Magazine, Spring 2016, Hardeman County Tourism Guide, page 13.

Crow era is a testament to the character and fortitude of my grandfather. Land ownership is a part of the "American dream." Land is a precious commodity. Its value constantly appreciates. One way of passing on a legacy from generation to generation is land ownership. The Robertson family is realizing this dream thanks to Crawford Robertson's vision.

I am aware of three homes that were built on the property during Crawford Robertson's lifetime. The original home was located several hundred feet from the home that I was familiar with as a young lad and grew up loving. This home still exists and currently has occupants. It was built in 1906 by my grandfather and another gentleman. The workmanship and design are still a marvel and still admired by many who are aware of its history. Its functionality has endured for 112 years. My Aunt Myrtle L. Robertson spent all of her ninety-five years in this home, with the exception of nine months. She died in 2002. Much more will be said about her later.

The front porch which faces what is now Newsom Road was a place of relaxation, conversation, and leisure. It also provided respite from a long day's work in the field. The lawn was adorned with stately shade trees. The swing brings back vivid memories. It was a place where on Sunday afternoons, I recall listening with my Uncle Johnny to Cardinals baseball games. Along with my two brothers, Darnell and James, he was an avid Yankees fan.

I was a Dodgers fan and still am to this day. As a child of the 40's Jackie Robinson was my hero. I grew up admiring him for his athletic skills and his ability to matriculate at predominately white UCLA as a three - sport athlete in the 1930s. His courage in the midst of adversity was an inspiration to me. In high school, I wrote my senior class paper on the life of Jackie Robinson. I still have that paper in my possession.

I fondly remember the Dodger lineups of the late 'forties and early 'fifties comprised of Jackie Robinson, Pee Wee Reese, Gil Hodges, Duke Snider, Roy Campanella, Carl Furillo, Billy Cox, Don Newcombe, and Joe Black. I also recall the legend of the Negro leagues and many of their great players: Satchel Paige, Josh Gibson, James Thomas "Cool Papa" Bell, and Buck Leonard, just to name a few. When the major leagues eliminated the color barrier, unfortunately, the Negro leagues soon folded.

In the early 'fifties, few blacks had televisions; Robert and Elma

Motley were exceptions. I remember walking a mile and a half to their home to watch the All-Star and World Series baseball games. Back to the home, I still recall one of the rooms being designated as the boys' room. This was obviously the room where all the boys spent much of their time: Guy, Johnny, Vivian, and Evelyn, my father.

I have fond memories of this home. Even though my parents, Evelyn and Pearl, lived in a residence two and a half miles away in the town of Whiteville, I spent a lot of time in this home. My brother Darnell and I slept in the boys' room where it was always a tug-of-war with the covers, particularly during the winter months.

This home was also a gathering place for the neighbors who wanted to listen to the Joe Louis fights in the 'thirties and 'forties. Few neighbors at this time had radios, so they would gather to support Joe Louis in his heavyweight fight battles. As a boy, I clearly remember the white picket fence that surrounded the home.

I built my home in rock-throwing distance from the 1906 home in 1964. I still reside in this home. The other home that was built on the farm was a tenant/sharecropper's home. This home was built in the early 'thirties. Much more will be said about this home later. I am told that this home was originally conceived as a home for my father and his family.

<h1 style="text-align:center">V</h1>

Role as Farmer/Entrepreneur and Visionary

THE ROBERTSON FAMILY FARM IS blessed with fertile soil which is great for crop production. Row cropping has been the major utilization for the acreage of this farm. Crops consisting of cotton, corn, soybeans, sorghum, milo, and peanuts were produced on this farm. Gardens were an annual staple for fresh vegetables and produce for healthy eating of seasonal items and supplied a canning operation to be used throughout the year. Two orchards were also on the farm, one of apples and one of pears. The orchards have long since disappeared, except for one pear tree remaining from its orchard. This tree is still producing and is more than a hundred years old.

Pastures for hay and livestock grazing are a part of the acreage. One pond exists. At one time, livestock consisted of cows, mules, horses, hogs, chickens, ducks, and turkeys. A smokehouse was used to store and preserve meat. I remember vividly large hams and shoulders hanging from the ceiling of the smokehouse. Late fall and early winter months were the time for hog killing. Fattened hogs were slaughtered for meat. The sausage, chitterlings, tenderloins, hams, shoulders, pig feet, and ears were all delights that came from the hog slaughter. I remember the huge black pots to boil the scalding water that were used to carry out this process. It took several men to carry out this process depending on the number of hogs to be slaughtered.

During hunting season, it was very common to take advantage of this opportunity to add to the table delicacies, pursuing the hunting of rabbits, squirrels, quail, etc. I also remember the hand-cranked ice cream maker. Homemade ice cream was always a welcome treat. The smells of cooking country ham, gravy, and biscuits remains vivid to me even to this day. As a young lad, I also remember milking the cows and helping to slop the hogs. Due to no indoor facilities, I also remember the outhouse, a staple at all homes during this era, particularly African American homes.

Crawford Robertson possessed a strong work ethic. This was evident in the success that he enjoyed as a producer and provider for his family. He was also concerned about his fellow-man. I recall a conversation that I had as a young man with Dr. Aubrey Richards, a local white family physician in Whiteville, where he shared with me the respect that citizens of the community had for my grandfather.

As a young man, I was reminded often of his efforts to start the day before daylight. He and his sons would assemble at the barn to harness and prepare the mules for the day's work. Often they would have to wait for sunlight before they could begin the day's work. Work often lasted from sunup to sundown.

Many farms of this era had a dinner bell that was used to signal time for lunch. This typically was around twelve noon. The wife or lady of the house was responsible for ringing the bell to indicate time for a break and time for a meal. My grandmother, Cora, was responsible for signaling this. A well-prepared sumptuous meal would be waiting. The dinner bell used in the 'twenties and 'thirties is posted in my backyard. It stands ready to be rung.

I might point out that the position of the sun was also used by many farmers to determine the time of day. If the sun was directly overhead, it was determined to be approximately noon. This sign indicated that it was time for a break.

In those years, water for drinking, cooking, and bathing on many farms typically came from a well or a cistern. Even though there once was a well, I remember most clearly the water drawn from a cistern. I can recall drinking cistern water from the water bucket, using a dipper.

The Robertson farm provided a source of livelihood not only for the Robertson family but also for sharecroppers and tenants who lived on the farm. A house built on the farm in the 1930s likely intended for my father served as a tenant's or sharecroppers' home. It was modestly built but representative of the era for sharecropper houses. Due to the death of the last tenant survivor, the home was demolished in 2018.

Tenants and Share Croppers known to have lived on the Robertson Farm included: Norman Rhodes and family, Early Hunter and family, Simon Vineyard and wife, Houston Harris and family, and A. J. Robertson. Several of these families moved on to own their own farms. A. J. Robertson, a cousin, was able to purchase a portion of the land that was once owned by my Uncle Johnny; in turn, I later purchased this land. A. J. resided in the tenant house until his death in 2016. At the time of the purchase, A. J. was promised use of this home for the duration of his life.

Sharecroppers received a portion of proceeds from the farm production based on an agreed arrangement with the owner. As a fourth-generation Robertson, I applaud my grandfather's wisdom and desire to help others. Many of them picked themselves up by their bootstraps and moved on to self-sufficiency.

Century Farm Certificate
Robertson Farm

Tennessee Historic Commission – National
Register of Historic Places Certificate.

VI

Educational Emphasis for Robertson Children

EDUCATION AND ACADEMIC PURSUIT HAVE been a trademark of the Robertson's from the early 1900s to the present. Crawford Robertson and his wife Cora were not educated in the formal sense of possessing diplomas or degrees. Both could minimally read or write. Keeping in mind that Crawford was born into slavery in 1856 and Cora, my grandmother, was born shortly thereafter in 1870, it is clear that their life experiences led them to see that education had value.

In the environment of the South in the late 1880s, blacks had very limited opportunity for education. For them, schooling beyond the eighth grade was nonexistent. Whatever education was available, the Robertson children took advantage of it with the encouragement and support of their parents. Remarkably, all six children raised to maturity received their eighth-grade training in the area. This was done even with the males juggling farm, work, and school.

After the eighth grade three of the Robertson children were sent away from home to attain high school diplomas in the early to mid-1920s: Vivian Lafayette, Myrtle Louise, and my father, Evelyn Crawford. Vivian and Myrtle were sent to Nashville to what was then A&I State College, now Tennessee State University. Nashville is 160 miles from Whiteville. A&I State College was a land grant college founded primarily for African Americans in 1912 that had a high school as a part of its college offerings. This was in the early to mid-nineteen twenties. Evelyn was younger and a few years later received his high school diploma from the Woodstock Training School in Lucy, Tennessee, which is in Shelby County, a few miles from Memphis, not far from Millington, and about sixty-five miles from Whiteville.

Under the circumstances of the times, I am amazed that Crawford and Cora had the foresight, audacity, vision, and inclination to send their children far distances from home to get a high school education. For many area families this was unthinkable, for many reasons. During this era less than 7 percent of African Americans attained a high school diploma. There was no opportunity for African Americans to pursue a high school education in Whiteville (Hardeman County) until 1929 due to segregation, when the Hardeman County Training School opened, later named the Allen-White High School.

Vivian later attended Lane College in Jackson, Tennessee. After high school graduation, Myrtle and Evelyn both attended A&I State College, where they both received degrees. Myrtle received a BS degree in home economics, and Evelyn received a BS degree in agriculture. After college both pursued their vocational paths. Myrtle enjoyed a forty-two-year career as a home economics instructor. All of her career was spent in Hardeman County. Forty of those years were at the school that her father Crawford helped to found. (More will be said about the school later.) She concluded her career in one of the two county high schools that had formerly been all-white, Central High School in Bolivar. In 1970, by federal court order all schools in Hardeman County were required to be desegregated. She was among several African American educators who integrated the faculty at Central High School. I was privileged to be a part of the faculty at Central, as vice-principal at that time. During her last two years of employment we worked there together. She retired in 1972.

My father pursued a career in education, where his first job was at Townsend High School in Winchester, Tennessee. Winchester was where I was born in 1941. He later taught in Lawrenceburg, Tennessee, and in Hardeman County. He also taught World II and Korean service veterans upon their discharge from the military. This initiative by the Veterans Administration supported their reintegration to the agrarian environment that they were returning to. He also worked for a period of time in the insurance industry.

Vivian, my uncle, worked as a farmer and spent most of his adult life in the timber or lumber industry.

My Uncle Johnny spent his entire life as a farmer and worked the Robertson Farm. He attained an eighth-grade education in the local school in Whiteville. Johnny was one of the first African Americans to own an automobile in Hardeman County—a Model T. Guy, the oldest of the Robertson clan, left the farm as a young man and spent his career in public utilities in Memphis. According to the 1930 census, his occupation was listed as a fireman. My aunt Elnora moved to Chicago as a young lady and spent the rest of her life there.

Sending his children away from home to attend school was a tremendous sacrifice for Crawford. Very few black families had either the inclination or the resources to do so. I know of only one other family in the Whiteville community to make this sacrifice during this era. Brother and sister Dan and Elma Greene also received this opportunity. Their parents sent them to Nashville for a high school education. I knew both of them, and they became highly productive citizens of the community upon their return: Dan as a brick mason and Elma as an educator. Dan and my Uncle Vivian were roommates in high school in Nashville.

In 1929, opportunities for African Americans to pursue a high school education in Hardeman County were made available. Crawford Robertson played an integral role in this endeavor.

VII

Role in Establishment of Secondary Education for Blacks in Hardeman County

THE EARLIEST KNOWN EFFORTS TO provide education for blacks began around 1905. Mr. Jesse C. Allen, a local educator, was the leader of the efforts to support schools for black children in the Whiteville Community. He utilized the local lodge hall to house the school. His efforts were very successful, and student numbers surpassed the capacity that the lodge hall could accommodate. Little financial support was provided by the local board of education so constant fundraising efforts were necessary on the part of the teachers and community to support the school. Mr. Allen's daughter, Hortense G. Norment, was my sixth-grade teacher. He had two other daughters who were teachers, Velma Seddens and Agatha Lake.

The Public-School Law of 1925 provided for a system of education, to consist of elementary and high schools as well as three state teacher's colleges. It was around this time that the Julius Rosenwald Foundation provided funds on a matching basis for Negro school buildings. Negro citizens purchased the land, and the Rosenwald Fund provided the building. The Whiteville Community qualified for this program.

The Hardeman County Training School was formed through the efforts of community leaders who worked tirelessly. They included Jesse C. Allen, Wm. Murphy, Dr. G. A. Shelton, Crawford Robertson, Isam Miller, J. N. Norment, Ed. Crisp, J. Wilson, H. McKinney, F. Baird, S.W.J. Allen, J. Reynolds, William Murphy, and J. H. White. My grandfather, Crawford Robertson, was the treasurer of this organization. J. H. White became principal due to the untimely death of Mr. Allen in 1921.

Crawford Robertson played an integral part in establishing opportunities for black youth to attain a high school education in the Whiteville, Hardeman County, community. The Hardeman County Training School was later named Allen-White High School in honor of Jesse Allen and James Herbert White.

The portion of the original building still standing includes the cornerstone, which identifies the names of the aforementioned individuals.

In 2004, Allen-White High School was nominated for designation as a State and National Historic Site by the Tennessee Historic Commission. This designation was awarded by the US Department of Interior in September 2004. Support for this nomination was provided by the Center for Historic Preservation from Middle Tennessee State University. Dr. Carroll Van West was instrumental in the application preparation and its ultimate designation. In one portion of the narrative, Dr. Van West referred to a farmer who reportedly had pledged $100 each year so long as the demand for the school warranted it. The farmer was later identified as Crawford Robertson, grandfather of the author.[5]

Maggie Neely, born in 1862 in Whiteville, Tennessee, was my great aunt. She was the half-sister of my grandfather Crawford. She was the daughter of Cornelia Robertson and Henry Neely. According to the 1930 census, she lived in what was referred to the Negro section of Whiteville. I now know that area to be Allen Street Extended. The census listed her occupation as manager of a rooming house which she owned. Other reports have her listed also as a teacher. She was single and head of the house. In 1930 she was sixty-eight years old.

Occupants in the rooming house were Augustus White, age 25; James H. White, 25; Algie Hopson, 20; Lou Ella Fitzgerald, 50; Ophelia Lockert, 28; Aeolian Lockert, 31; Aeolian Lockert, 2; and Leonard Lockert, 0.

Two years earlier, James H. White had moved to Whiteville from Gallatin, Tennessee. He was one half of the namesake of the Allen-White High School, formerly the Hardeman County Training School (HCTS). James White's wife, Augustus, was my kindergarten and first grade teacher. I entered the first grade in 1946. She was an adorable lady and revered by many.

---

[5] Evelyn C. Robertson Jr. *Education and the American Dream: The Allen-White School Story 1905–1970* (Booksurge.Com, 2009), pages 6, 8–9, 72.

There is a distinct irony in the revelation of this research. This residence was where I grew up. Little did I know of its rich history prior to my discovery of the1930 census. The residence was willed to my uncle Vivian Lafayette Robertson by my great aunt Maggie Neely at her death. My parents resided there until my mother, Pearl Robertson, built a residence at 225 Jackson St.

The accomplishments and achievement of James H. White are documented in my book, *Education and the American Dream: The Allen-White School Story, 1905–1970*, published in 2009. Suffice it to say, James H. White used his Allen-White experience in Whiteville as a springboard for greater things. From 1948 to 1950 he served as president of Lane College in Jackson, Tennessee, and later was the founding president of what is now Mississippi Valley State University in Itta Bena, Mississippi, where he served for many years until his retirement.

VIII

Educational/Professional Pursuits and Successes of Children, Grandchildren, and Great Grandchildren of Crawford Robertson

REFERENCE HAS BEEN MADE TO the educational and professional pursuits of Crawford's children. His grandchildren and great grandchildren have also taken seriously the role that education can play in building success and realizing ways of serving humankind. Four of Crawford's grandchildren received college degrees; the author and first cousin Vivian Lafayette Robertson Jr. attained master's degrees and served as educators and administrators. I will talk more about my career later. My two brothers, Darnell and James received college degrees from Tennessee State University and served long careers in their chosen fields. My two children, Jeffrey and Sheila both attained college degrees: Jeffrey received a BS in criminal justice from Tennessee State University, and Sheila earned degrees from the University of Tennessee and Kent State University, and a doctoral degree in physical therapy from Rocky Mountain University. Darnell's children, Darnella and Steven, both attained degrees, Darnella, a law degree and Steven, a bachelor's degree in sociology. My cousin Vivian Lafayette's son Daniel also attained a college degree.

My grandson Malik is a 2019 graduate of Middle Tennessee State University. He is a fourth generation Robertson to earn a college degree. His degree is in agribusiness. My granddaughter Jasmine is a 2020 graduate at the same university, majoring in social work. My brother

James's children, Jennifer and Aaron, both attended college, and Jennifer attained an associate's degree.

Steven's daughter Cheyenne is currently a college student.

My uncle Guy and his wife Neila were the parents of four children, Elvesta, Claude, Pearl, and Guy Jr. Guy's children are my first cousins. They are all high school graduates who grew up in Memphis and graduated from Manassas High School.

Guy was the eldest of Crawford and Cora's children. He matriculated to Memphis as a young man and instilled the importance of education to his children. Several of his grandchildren pursued higher education. Elvesta and his wife, Ann, were the parents of Elvesta Jr., Elizabeth Ann, Henry Dewey, Ray Anthony, Audfrey Guy, and William Mose. Their children matriculated at the following colleges and universities: Memphis State (University of Memphis), Jackson State University, Lemoyne-Owen, Arkansas AM&N (Arkansas Pine Bluff), and Bishop.

Little is known about my cousin Pearl and her children, I am aware of two of her children, Fred and McClennan. I am aware that there were two children born to the union with her husband Herman Jackson. I do not know their names. Claude and his wife Ruth are the parents of Claudia, Jean, and Skip. The author is not aware of their professions or vocational pursuits.

Guy Jr. and his wife, Louise, are the parents of Shirley, Eleanor, Madolyn, Ronald, Guy Jr., Brenda, Janet, and Marcellus. Each of them pursued their own professional and vocational goals.

Suffice it to say that education has been rigorously pursued by the Robertson family and has paid dividends. The family has benefited magnificently, and so has society. We may not be the brightest stars in the galaxy, but with hard work, determination, persistence, and perseverance, much is possible, as proven by the Robertson family.

The author was born in Winchester, Tennessee, on November 19, 1941, to Evelyn C. Robertson Sr. and Pearl Brewer Robertson. Winchester is located in middle Tennessee in Franklin County. Winchester is where my father was employed as a teacher at Townsend High School. This was his first job out of college (A&I State College in Nashville, now Tennessee State University). He taught agriculture and coached basketball. My father later worked at a school in Lawrenceburg, also in middle Tennessee.

I have to assume that my father was working his way back to West Tennessee, where our family has its roots, and he moved to Memphis, where he worked in the insurance industry.

By this time the family had grown. On May 17, 1943, my brother Darnell was born. We moved to Whiteville to a home that was owned by my uncle Vivian Lafayette. This home was formerly owned by my great aunt, Maggie Neely. Maggie was the half- sister of my grandfather Crawford. Maggie by will and deed transferred this property to my uncle Vivian. My brother James Albert was born in this home on October 28, 1949. My mother lived in this home until the early 'seventies when she built a residence across the street at 225 Jackson St., where she lived until her death in 1999.

After moving back to Whiteville, my father taught at the Campbell School in Whiteville and later worked with a government program to assimilate returning World II veterans and Korean War veterans back in the agrarian society from which they left to assume their military obligation, which had changed to some degree upon their return. They were taught agriculture science, business, and crop production. These veterans were beneficiaries of the GI Bill, and many used this benefit to not only support their families but to seek opportunities for self-sufficiency. This training enabled them to be more knowledgeable of the agriculture and farming industry.

My father was the victim of a homicide on July 16, 1955. This tragedy created a tremendous challenge for my mother, Pearl, with three boys to raise, ages 14, 12, and 6. It was a time fraught with fear, trepidation, and uncertainty. This was a dark moment for the Robertson family. Even with the pride of other Robertson successes and achievements, this tragedy created a pause and a need for reflection. It required looking inward and to seek God's intervention. Through faith and through our Christian ideals, God answered our prayers. My aunt Myrtle, a person of faith and a pillar of strength played a tremendous role in the lives of my brothers and me. In her own way she not only supported us but supported my mother as well. Each of us owe a tremendous debt of gratitude and thanks to her. Our educational support and pursuits can be attributed to her. I think of her daily because of her sacrifices and love.

My mother Pearl, a gentle, loving, kind, caring, and supportive person, gave us the nurturing that we needed to go forward and to stake out our place in this global society. She enjoyed a twenty-plus-year career as the cafeteria manager at the Allen-White High School. She was renowned for her culinary skills, and even today people talk about the great food that she prepared. She also served several years as the nutrition coordinator at the Whiteville Senior Citizens Center. Allen-White is the school where my brothers and I matriculated. This is also the school that my grandfather was instrumental in helping to found. It is also the school where my aunt Myrtle taught for forty years as a home economics instructor. It is also the school where I was employed as a teacher and coach. Allen-White was rock-throwing distance from our residence.

There is a cliché that says it takes a village to raise a child. I believe that the village in Whiteville, Tennessee, was very beneficial in our nurturing and growth. I will name some names later, but the role of the Elcanaan Baptist Church, under the pastorate of Rev. L. Nelson, the Boy Scouts under the leadership of Jesse I. Norment and Charlie N. Stallings, and the school athletic opportunities were very meaningful. My brothers and I played basketball and baseball and each acknowledged as excellent athletes. These activities were great character and confidence builders. I even had an opportunity to go to a St. Louis Cardinal tryout camp. My position of choice was third base. My brother Darnell played outfield and pitched, and James played outfield. I had the opportunity to coach James in basketball and baseball at the high school level.

I entered first grade in 1946. My first-grade teacher was Mrs. Augustus White, the wife of the high school principal, J. H. White. She also served as the elementary school principal. She was an adorable, strict, but loving individual and was admired by all. I think of her even to this day and the impact that she had on my life at such an early stage. She and her husband lived in the rooming house owned by my great aunt Maggie Neely which was adjacent to the Allen-White campus.

Village supporters and mentors in addition to the ones mentioned were Major Jarrett, high school principal; E. L. Rivers, teacher and coach and businessman; Minerva Jarrett, Lillie N. Rivers, and H. G. Norment, teachers; Dan Greene and Blanche Greene, church members; Bernice D. Stallings and Elma Motley, teachers; R. B. Motley, businessman; and Alexander Sanders, Margaret Sanders, and Morris Parham, teachers.

What these all had in common was that they were members of the Elcanaan Baptist Church. E. L. Rivers was board chairman at Elcanaan Baptist Church, the position that I now hold.

As a youth, I gained much inspiration from frequent and sometimes weekly reading of African American newspapers such as the *Pittsburgh Courier*, *The Afro-American*, *The Chicago Defender*, and *The Tri-State Defender*. These newspapers provided stories of African Americans succeeding in business, entertainment, and sports. These newspapers highlighted the many injustices prevalent in our society during that era, as well as calling for change. Such articles and stories were not a part of the mainstream media, and rarely did a positive story of African American achievements find its way into their bylines or stories. My brother Darnell during his high school years had a regular route for weekend distribution of *The Chicago Defender* to local citizens in our community. This likely incited his entrepreneurial interest. I also valued *Ebony* and *Jet* magazines growing up as a child, as they were great inspirations as well. Even in the digital age, I still prefer the print edition of newspapers.

At seventeen years of age, I graduated from the Allen-White High School. Before entering college, I assumed my first job at the Peabody Hotel in Memphis, Tennessee. Between May and August of 1959, I worked at the Peabody. My cousin George Gilchrist at that time had worked at the Peabody thirty-four years and was instrumental in getting me a job as an elevator operator. The three and a half months at the Peabody was a great experience. The responsibility of a job, the ability to earn my own money, and the people contacts all resonated positively with me.

The Peabody Hotel was and still is a premiere hotel in Memphis and the South. Big bands performed nightly in the Skyway where the who's who of Memphis would come for entertainment dressed in finery and splendor. Being impressionable at this stage of my life, I was very impressed with the crowd that traveled each night on my elevator. My appetite for big band and jazz music was whetted through this experience.

During those three and a half months, I stayed with my uncle Vivian and his family. I commuted from his home on College Street by street bus to the hotel each day. Earnings from work I used to buy clothes and other necessities for college.

In August of 1959, I entered A&I State College (Tennessee State

University) in Nashville. As I boarded the train for the six-hour trek to Nashville, I certainly felt the butterflies and the anxiety of facing college life as a young teenager. The uncertainty of the unknown was very apparent as I moved to this new stage of my life. I obviously had the awareness that my father, two aunts, and an uncle before me had faced similar challenges.

I soon settled into the rigors of college life. Being embraced by fellow classmates and other Hardeman Countians aided in the transition from the small town of Whiteville to the second largest city in the state of Tennessee and the setting of a vibrant college community. I quickly had to learn the value of time management, discipline, and personal responsibility.

Tennessee State University was founded in 1912 as an institution to serve primarily African Americans. Its mission has changed with the times and is multicultural and racially diverse. It now is considered one of the leading HBCUs (historically black colleges and universities) in the nation.

In early 1960 students from North Carolina A&T University in Greensboro began protests addressing racial segregation in public accommodations. Stores such as Woolworth and Kress were targets. These protests quickly spread throughout the South and college students at black colleges and universities using sit-ins became the catalyst for the development of organizations to promote the civil rights movement of the 1960s. Students at Tennessee State University, Fisk, Meharry, and American Baptist Theological Seminary were willing participants in the movement.

During my first two years at TSU I spent a lot of time attending mass meetings, which were almost daily, and participating in marches. This movement helped me quickly realize that the separate but equal doctrine had no place in our society (*Plessy v. Ferguson*).

During my tenure at Tennessee State University I had the opportunity to march with civil rights icons such as John Lewis and Diane Nash. They were students at sister colleges in Nashville at this time. The student protest leadership at Tennessee State University was aggressive and persistent. Two fellow Hardeman County students who were intricately involved in the movement were Curtis Murphy and Lester McKinnie (aka El-Senzengakulu Zulu), Curtis from Whiteville and Zulu from Bolivar.

I considered the protest efforts not as a distraction in my college life but as a defining opportunity to soul search, build character, and attempt to right the wrongs that were so evident in our society. As I have pursued life after college, those experiences emboldened me and gave me courage to forge ahead regardless of the obstacles.

Maintaining my focus to get a college education was paramount, with the encouragement and support of my family. With two brothers behind me, it was my goal to move to the next stage as rapidly as possible. I attained my degree in political science in three years. One of my defining experiences at Tennessee State University was as a delegate in 1961 attending a Little United Nations Convention at Indiana University in Bloomington with two other fellow students and Professor Cornelius Jones, instructor in the Political Science Department. Collegians from all across the US were in attendance. This was a tremendous experience and further opened my eyes as to the possibilities associated with this global society. As president of the Town Hall Association at TSU, I had the opportunity to install the president of the student government in 1962. Shortly later, at the age of twenty, I ventured to the see what the next chapter of life would bring.

In 1962, the *Brown v. Board of Education* decision was seven years old, but little effort had been instituted to make its findings a reality in much of the South. The separate but equal doctrine of *Plessy v. Ferguson* was still the de facto law of the land, particularly in the South.

The struggle for voting rights, equality in education, and jobs was a continuous focus of the early 'sixties and 'seventies. Organizations such as the NAACP, SCLC, National Urban League, SNCC, and their leaders played a significant role in the progress of minimizing barriers that stood in the way of the US Constitution's vision of equality for all of its citizens. The 1964 Voting Rights Act was a positive step in this nation's movement to inclusion in the process fundamental to all citizens, the right to vote without restrictions or barriers such as race, creed, color, etc. Unfortunately, today voting rights are under attack in many areas through suppression.

As I attempted to move my professional and vocational trajectory forward, I observed the national, state, and local challenges that persisted in this nation. Living in a small, rural setting there was much opposition to the direction that the nation appeared to be moving toward. Local leaders, businessmen, landowners, and education leaders were determined to maintain the status quo. This opposition was obviously for personal, cultural, and financial reasons. In their view, separation of the races was the way things were supposed to be. Some even used the Bible to justify the arrangement. The courts, to their credit, played a huge role in breaking some of these barriers.

In Hardeman County, the federal court in one of its decisions struck down the dual system of education that had existed since the Plessy decision supported separate but equal. In 1970 schools in Hardeman County were no longer identified by race.

As I returned to Whiteville in August 1962, I was immediately hired by the Hardeman County school system as a teacher and was assigned to Allen-White High School. This is the high school that I graduated from in 1959. Mr. Major Jarrett was principal at Allen-White and remained at Allen-White until its closure in 1970. I taught seventh and eighth grades health and science, world history, and driver's education and coached boys' basketball.

On October 13, 1963, I married Hugholene Ellison, a native of Toone, Tennessee, and a fellow educator in the Hardeman County school system. We have enjoyed fifty-seven years of marriage and are the parents of two children, Jeffrey and Sheila.

In the summer of 1966, I was fortunate to be selected to participate in an NDEA Institute at Southwest Missouri State University, as it was known at that time. Southwest Missouri State is located in Springfield. Our daughter, Sheila, was born while I was in Springfield. This institute was a federal program and was designed to help social science educators better understand the complexity of the global world that we were living in. Russia, just a few years earlier, had launched Sputnik, and the space race had begun. The biweekly stipend associated with this eight-week program was very helpful in putting food on the table for my growing family as well as enhancing me intellectually. The twenty-nine other educators in this program represented a diverse mix of cultures and localities and proved to be very helpful for me as I looked to the future. This group was very collegial.

After earning my master's degree in 1969 from Tennessee State University, I was appointed principal of the Allen-White Elementary School. This was grades K–6. Allen-White Elementary was located on the same campus as the high school in a modern building that had been constructed in 1964. I succeeded Mrs. C. Elma Motley in this role upon her retirement from the school system. Mrs. Motley and Mr. Jarrett were members of the Elcanaan Baptist Church and were role models. Elcanaan was a beacon in our community within the religious circles. It is located adjacent to the Allen-White school campus on Jackson and Allen Street Extended.

My tenure at Allen-White Elementary School was brief due to the Federal Court Order issued by Federal Judge Herman McCrae that the Hardeman County Schools must immediately desegregate. This decision was handed down in 1969.

During the school year 1970, a new era of education in Hardeman County was embarked upon. In the early stages of education Hardeman County had gone from approximately sixty schools to now nine schools.

In 1970, due to court order, there were three schools in Bolivar, one in Whiteville, one in Grand Junction, one in Toone, two in Middleton, and one in Hornsby. Two high schools survived the court order: Central High School in Bolivar and Middleton High School in Middleton. Prior to the court order there were six high schools, and a dual school system essentially existed.

Due to the desegregation, fourteen African American educators were assigned to Central High School, and proportionate numbers were assigned to the other schools based on established ratios. I was assigned to Central High School as vice-principal, the first African American to be appointed in such a role in a majority white school. My aunt Myrtle, who had at that time worked forty years at Allen-White, was assigned to Central as home economics instructor. She retired in 1972, concluding an illustrious career. In 2013, she was posthumously inducted into the Tennessee State University Agriculture and Home Economics Hall of Fame.

The 1970 school year in Hardeman County was marked with much anxiety. Never before had such an undertaking as merging schools taken place. Racial makeup at Central was close to fifty–fifty white to black. Amazingly, the school year proceeded exceedingly well. There were few issues. Occasionally, there was a bomb threat, but that's all it was—a threat. There were occasional fights but nothing that was unusual.

I attribute the success of the early years of desegregation in this school setting to the tone that was set by the principal Milton Basden, and myself. He was an excellent educator, a no-nonsense person with a reputation as a strict disciplinarian. I too was a disciple of this philosophy. In our initial meeting after my appointment, we agreed that we would work together and not let issues that we faced separate us, particularly based on race. Obviously, we were challenged, but we stayed true to our agreement. Central High School served as a model for West Tennessee as to the relationship between the races and educational success of all students. We were seen in the community together, at athletic events, home and away.

In 1972, I am certain that based on Mr. Basden's recommendation, the Hardeman County Jaycees recognized me as Outstanding Educator of the Year. I attribute the four years that I worked at Central High School in Bolivar as being pivotal to many of my future opportunities and successes.

In 1974, while working at Central High School I was invited to attend a meeting at Western Mental Health Institute, the psychiatric hospital in Bolivar. This meeting involved community leaders and hospital officials addressing the need to form a community council to address issues and challenges facing those with mental illness. This meeting was coordinated by Hospital Superintendent Dr. Earl Ninow.

A few weeks after the meeting at the hospital, I received a telephone call from Dr. Ninow. He informed me of a job opportunity at Western and inquired of my interest. I remember this very distinctly; it was in February of 1974. I informed him that I was under contract through the rest of the school year and would not be able to make a change of employment until the school year ended. I did say to him that I would certainly give some thought to this idea and thanked him for this gesture. Weeks and months went by, and I had no further contact with Dr. Ninow.

On about May 20, 1974, I contacted him to see if the job opportunity that he described was still available. He informed me that it was. After further discussion, he offered me the job and asked if I could be available June 1. I informed him that I could. The position offered was Assistant Superintendent for Community Services. Even with no formal training in behavioral health, I still felt confident of my administrative skills and felt that I could succeed in this arena. I resigned my position with the school system and focused my attention on this new venture.

The decision to leave the school was not an easy decision. I was very comfortable in the school system setting and felt that there would be further opportunities if I chose to stay. Art Browder was Superintendent of Schools in Hardeman County at the time of my resignation. I remember him saying to me that if I ever wanted to return to the school system the opportunity would be there. This was certainly reassuring, and I really appreciated it. As I went forward, this was my ace in the hole.

I was intrigued by the opportunity to take on a new challenge of assuming the role as an administrator/ assistant superintendent in a psychiatric hospital setting. Western Mental Health Institute was located approximately twelve miles from my home. Later, I learned that there were doomsayers and skeptics predicting my quick demise in this setting and my eventual return to the educational system.

On June 1, 1974, I reported to work at Western Mental Health Institute. I had never remotely thought about the possibility of working at this agency of state government. In my travels from Whiteville to Bolivar, I had to pass by Western every time. The architecture, the stately buildings, and the landscape expanse were all very impressive, not to mention the history of services to the mentally ill population provided since 1886. I was convinced that I had made the right decision to join the staff there. However, I would be less than truthful, if I said that I did not have some anxiety about the decision.

The first six months at Western were trying and challenging. Due to the political atmosphere in employment in state jobs in state agencies in Tennessee at that time, it was not uncommon to encounter political interference. It was less common in professional positions, but occasionally it occurred at that level as well. That was certainly the case at this time in 1974. Within six months after my decision to move to this job, the person responsible for my hiring, the superintendent, was under attack from the local patronage committee. This attack was due to his refusal to hire or fire people that he deemed inappropriate. The patronage committee were local supporters of the party in power that had no authority other than they wanted certain individuals hired often, whether they had qualifications or not. Typically, these individuals were loyal and had influence with the party in power. They also targeted individuals that they wanted fired for the same reason.

As an assistant superintendent, I was one of four professionals who made up the management team of the facility. The management team included the superintendent, the Assistant Superintendent of Administrative Services, the Assistant Superintendent for Clinical Services, and the Assistant Superintendent for Community Services. The departments under my supervision included social work, psychology, adjunctive therapy, chaplaincy, and outpatient services. I also served as liaison to the Community Mental Health Centers serving this twenty-one-county area of West Tennessee. They were beginning to take on a larger role in serving individuals who were being discharged from the hospital.

In January or February 1975, the superintendent was terminated by the governor. The commissioner of the Department of Mental Health and Mental Retardation was Dr. Harold Jordan. Dr. Jordan was the first African American resident physician at Vanderbilt University Medical Center, completing his residency between 1964 and 1967 and as commissioner was instrumental in supporting my hiring at Western Mental Health Institute. The governor was Ray Blanton.

Chaos, confusion and anxiety reigned for many months. Immediately after the termination of the superintendent, the Assistant Superintendent for Administrative Services resigned in protest. One interim superintendent after another was a fact of life for months after the termination. Rumors, uncertainty, and lack of a coherent direction were readily apparent.

In 1976, Dr. Morris Cohen from Memphis, Tennessee, was appointed superintendent. His tenure was short. He was terminated in 1978. Dr. William Jennings succeeded him.

Dr. Earl Ninow later returned to work at the Tennessee Department of Mental Health at the central office in Nashville, serving in a clinical role and simultaneously providing psychiatric consultation to residents at the Nat T. Winston Developmental Center in Bolivar for several years. He also served as a surveyor for the Joint Commission for the Accreditation of Hospitals.

In June 1979, I was appointed by the Commissioner of Mental Health and Mental Retardation, Dr. James Brown, as Superintendent of the yet-to-be-named Dual Diagnosis Facility that was to be located on the

Western Mental Health Institute grounds but would be a separate facility. Assistant Commissioner Dr. James Foshee was my immediate supervisor. Lamar Alexander was governor of the state at this time.

The facility had 150 beds and was statewide, serving individuals that had developmental and psychiatric disabilities. Many were already housed in state developmental and or psychiatric facilities served by the Tennessee Department of Mental Health and Mental Retardation. This facility was later named the Nat T. Winston Developmental Center. It was named after the former commissioner of the department, psychiatrist Dr. Nat T. Winston.

June 1979 was filled with building modification, employee recruitment, orientation, and training. During the training and orientation, there was a court challenge to the appropriateness of such a facility. This challenge was instigated by an advocacy group from North Carolina. Tennessee's position prevailed, and the facility opened on time.

The first resident arrived at the facility on July 1, 1979. I hired the entire complement of employees to staff this facility. I might point out that this was done with no outside interference or questions. I think this points out the progress that had been made over the past years in that regard.

My first hire was Julia Gallaher, as she was at that time. She was hired as the Assistant Superintendent for Residential Services. Other early hires included social worker Carolyn Nolan, Director of Standards Russell Pete Davidson, Fiscal Director Larry Anderson, and directors Pat Pope and Robert Word. Clerical support was provided by Evelyn Vanderberghe and Vernet Duncan. Evelyn accompanied me to my next assignment and was a very loyal, competent, and dedicated employee. Many of the developmental technicians were recruited from Western and were psychiatric technicians in that setting.

My four years as superintendent at the Nat T. Winston Developmental Center were challenging and transformative. My administration and staff were determined to provide a model of care for this population that was caring, compassionate, nurturing, and appropriate for their specific needs. Due to their dual diagnosis this wasn't always easy. I was proud that as a result of the services provided, many were able to be transitioned to community settings.

The hallmark of any facility or organization is to be recognized by its peers regionally and nationally. After two years of operation we applied for accreditation from the American Association for Individuals with Developmental Disabilities (AAIDD). Accreditation was awarded and retained throughout the history of the institution.

In June 1983, I was appointed superintendent of Western Mental Health Institute, located in Bolivar. This appointment was due to the resignation of Dr. William Jennings. Keep in mind that the Nat T. Winston Developmental Center and Western Mental Health Institute were both located on the same campus. It meant for me literally walking across the street.

I was the first superintendent appointed at Western Mental Health Institute who had neither medical nor clinical background. I served at Western from 1983 to 1991. Accreditation, which was first attained in 1975 during my tenure there as an assistant superintendent, was maintained during my tenure as superintendent. I attribute familiarity with the institution and staff familiarity with me along with my management style as factors in any success that I experienced during my tenure in this setting.

One significant achievement beyond the level of care provided to the patients was the publishing of the history of the institution, *Grains of Sand: A History of Western Mental Health Institute 1886–1986*. With cooperation of the local banks of Hardeman County, the cost of publishing the book was underwritten. The limited copies produced were exhausted rapidly. There are still inquiries as to the book's availability. Institute Board of Trustees Chair Susan Anderson coordinated the activities of the committee that developed the history.

Deinstitutionalization was a process that was very much in focus during my tenure at Western, and the number of beds rapidly decreased. The ability to depopulate the state institutions was directly related to the availability of community resources to support and sustain former patients in community settings. This concept was a national movement and very controversial in many areas of the country. Where supports were available and services existed, this concept was preferable to institutionalization and in some instances much cheaper. Community services through networks such as Community Mental Health Centers play a huge role in services to this population in the community. Private as well as other public resources address the needs of this population in the community as well; when they are coordinated, citizens with mental illness win.

During my tenure at Western the population was reduced from 750 beds to approximately 580. Today, it has approximately 140 beds. What happened? I will address that later.

The original Western campus was stately; its architecture was captivating, surrounded by trees and multiple buildings. At one time it housed as many as twenty-five hundred patients. It was also known as home to a colony of albino squirrels. The sight of these squirrels created much interest to employees and visitors alike.

Most of the late 1800s psychiatric hospitals had a unique mystique about them, and Western was no exception. Its farm and dairy operation were an integral part of operations for many years. Its postal services, water and fire services, and security services made it very much a self-contained community, to some degree independent of the town of Bolivar.

I enjoyed my tenure at Western Mental Health Institute. It carried with it the stresses of any position of its type but was an opportunity for rewarding experiences where lives of patients were impacted for good and the lives of employees serving the needs of this population were impacted as well. In many ways I thought this might be where I would retire. While serving as superintendent at Western, I also served for nine months as interim superintendent at Memphis Mental Health Institute in Memphis simultaneously with my role at Western. There was a vacancy at that institution, and I was asked to fill in until a replacement could be secured. In 1990 with my combined work as an educator and my eighteen years at that time working for the Tennessee Department of Mental Health and Mental Retardation, I was approaching thirty years of service to the state of Tennessee and was a vested participant in the Tennessee Consolidated Retirement System.

In December of 1990, I received a call from Governor Ned McWherter's office indicating that he was considering a change in his commissioner of Mental Health and Mental Retardation and would like for me to consider assuming this position. In November he had just been reelected to his second term as governor of the state of Tennessee.

To say that I was surprised by this call is an understatement. It was earthshaking. It meant changes, family adjustments and it meant the need to relocate. It also meant some self- introspection. Was I willing to accept the rigors of this role? Was I up to this task? As a professional, I never lacked confidence. I grew up being self-assured. I had encountered many challenges up to this point in my life. To be leader of a statewide agency responsible for a sixty-million-dollar budget and thousands of employees as a member of a governor's cabinet was taking this to another level.

Deciding to accept this offer meant prayer, solitude, and consultation with my wife Hugholene. She was well advanced in her career as an educator and was nearing retirement. It also meant support and endorsement from my mother, Pearl, and my aunt Myrtle, who both were advancing in age and experiencing some health issues. I deemed my presence in the area as a support mechanism for the two of them. After a family conference when I explained to them the opportunity that I had and the historic significance of this moment, they expressed unanimity in favor of my accepting this role. My brother Darnell who was visiting from Ohio was present at this meeting.

Taking this job meant moving to Nashville, the state capital. My wife opted not to disrupt her career as a teacher in Whiteville, as she was nearing retirement. This meant that I had to go apartment shopping.

I located an apartment in downtown Nashville, the Riverfront Apartments, located on First Avenue, with a view of the Cumberland River. It was less than five minutes from my office. I resided there the four years that I served as commissioner. This view represented solemnity and therapy for a challenging position.

To maintain my community presence, I returned home each weekend during my four-year tenure, attending Elcanaan Baptist Church on Sunday and participating in the monthly board meetings of the Bank of Bolivar, where I served as a director. During the summers when school was out, Hugholene would join me in Nashville; however, we would return home each weekend.

Serving as commissioner of a state agency carries with it administrative and ceremonial responsibilities. It also requires the development and promulgation of policies that conform to the goals and vision of the administration that you are serving. The commissioner is the administration's voice to the citizens to convey what it is attempting to do to serve the citizens' needs and to serve these needs in a morally and fiscally responsible manner. State agencies have varying constituencies, and those constituencies desire input, and their needs and advocacy must be respected. Balancing expectations of advocacy groups against what was feasible and possible often became challenging. This was particularly true as it relates to dollars and cents.

If there was an advantage that I had in assuming this job, it was that I had served in positions that affected both population groups which were identified in the name of our department: the mentally ill and now the intellectually disabled, formerly known as the mentally retarded. I might point out that due to the magnitude and complexity of the needs and challenges of the population served during my tenure, the department has now been divided. There now exist two state departments focusing on the population groups.

The legal challenges to the existence of institutions versus community alternatives to serve the mentally ill and intellectually disabled occupied a lot of my time as commissioner. These challenges had local roots from advocacy groups and soon gained support from the federal government, and thus the lawsuits ensued. This phenomenon was part of a national trend that up to the 'nineties had somewhat escaped Tennessee. Today there are no state facilities operated by the state of Tennessee that serve the mentally retarded (intellectually disabled),

On the mental health side of the department, there was no shortage of issues and challenges either. Balancing the allocation of funds between the institutions and the community to best serve the needs of the mentally ill was not only challenging but very difficult. Aged facilities were also a concern and had to be addressed. Plans and construction were begun on two facilities during my tenure as commissioner. The Harold Jordan Facility on the Clover Bottom Developmental Center Grounds was begun as well as the Middle Tennessee Mental Health Institute, both in Nashville.

To address the issue of service allocation and funding, the department with the support of the administration ventured to develop a master plan for mental health service delivery. This venture required input from advocates, consumers, and professionals. Consultants from throughout the country knowledgeable of mental health delivery at the community and institutional level were brought to Tennessee to work with the committee organized to develop the master plan. Funding was provided to support the committee's needs and efforts and to bring in the consultants. After a yearlong effort and much input, a plan was ultimately developed. This plan provided a blueprint for service delivery for the mentally ill in Tennessee beginning in 1994. This plan required many years of implementation due to funding and resource development, and I am certain that some elements are being refined even today. I consider the mental health master plan as the single most important achievement of my administration as commissioner.

During my tenure as commissioner of the Department of Mental Health and Mental Retardation I was elected as president of the National Organization of Mental Health Commissioners. This organization is known as the National Association of State Mental Health Program Directors (NASMHPD). It is comprised of commissioners/directors from throughout the United States including Guam. It was quite an honor to chair this organization. I remember distinctly at one of the meetings having the opportunity to introduce Tipper Gore, wife of US Vice President Albert Gore to this group for remarks. She was a strong advocate for mental health services, not only in Tennessee but throughout the nation. Having the respect and support of your peers was very meaningful to me.

My tenure as commissioner ended in January 1995, which coincided with the end of Ned McWherter's second term as governor. I will forever be indebted to Governor McWherter for his confidence and support. Serving as commissioner was the highlight and crowning honor of my career.

Governor Don Sunquist succeeded Governor McWherter. He appointed me to chair the Title 33 Revision Commission. The mandate of this commission was to perform a comprehensive review of Title 33 and to make recommendations to revise it. Title 33 represented the laws governing services to the mentally ill and mentally retarded/intellectually and developmentally disabled in the state of Tennessee as codified by the state. This report, which included input from hundreds of Tennesseans, was submitted to the governor in January 2000.

Following my twenty-two-year career with the Tennessee Department of Mental Health and Mental Retardation, I worked one year as Vice-President for Behavioral Health at West Tennessee Health

Care in Jackson, Tennessee. In 1996, I was offered an opportunity to serve as executive director of the Southwest Tennessee Development District. This eight-county development district provided economic and community development services. It also served as the area agency for aging services for this eight-county area as well. I retired from the development district in August of 2007 after serving there eleven years—thus concluding a forty-five-year career as an educator, mental health administrator, and economic and community development professional.

In my retirement I have continued to be engaged in civic, community, and fraternal activities. I am now serving on boards and committees, many related to service entities that I was involved with in my professional life. Some of these organizations include St. John's Community Services Board of Directors, the Hardeman County Community Health Center Board of Directors, the 100 Black Men of West Tennessee, the local chapter of the Association for the Preservation of Tennessee Antiquities (APTA), and the Quinco Mental Health Center Board of Directors.

Quinco Mental Health Center was founded at Western Mental Health Institute. It originated out of the outpatient department of Western. It was formed to serve the community mental health needs of a five-county area: Hardeman, Chester, Decatur, Hardin, and McNairy Counties. In a board of directors meeting in 1974 in my office in the Clement Building at Western, Quinco was given its name: Quin (five) Co (County). Mrs. Inez Brisendine, a board member and director of the Hardeman County Welfare Agency, coined that name, and it was readily adopted. Quinco continues to address mental health and behavioral health needs of these counties and has expanded to other locations. From 1974 to 1975, I served in a dual role as interim director at Quinco and assistant superintendent at Western. I am proud to now serve on its board of directors. As life would have it, I have come full circle.

Unveiling of sign commemorating the opening of the
Nat T. Winston Developmental Center-pictured Dr. Nat
Winston, Governor Lamar Alexander, Senator John Wilder,
Dr. James Brown, Evelyn Robertson & others.

Evelyn Robertson Jr., presenting Governor Ned McWherter
a copy of the Book, "Grains of Sand," the history of
Western Mental Health Institute 1886-1986.

Evelyn Robertson & James Sanderson at the Tennessee State Capitol
at the inauguration of Governor Ned McWherter, January 1991.

I am also a 33° Degree Prince Hall Mason and a life member of Kappa
Alpha Psi Fraternity, Inc. I am also a founding member of the Southwest
Tennessee Landowners Organization. This organization focuses on the
interests and opportunities for minority landowners in Hardeman and
surrounding counties. I am also a life member of the NAACP and the
Tennessee State University National Alumni Association.

In my professional and vocational endeavors, I have received
numerous awards and recognitions. To list a few, in 2010 I received the
Humanitarian of the Year Award from the ARC of the Mid-South at its
fifteenth Annual Benefit Gala. In 2013, I was awarded the Pillow Lee
Award by the St. John's Community Services Organization. In February
2017 I was honored as a Living Legend by the Tennessee College of
Applied Technology of Whiteville, Tennessee.

On May 27, 2018, at the fifty-fifth Annual Freedom Fund Banquet of
the Jackson-Madison County NAACP, I was recognized as a Legend and
inducted into the NAACP Gallery of Legends. In 2018, I was awarded
the Lifetime Achievement Award by the Tennessee Community
Organizations (TNCO) at its annual conference. Also, in 2018 I was
awarded the Albert Nelson Marquis Lifetime Achievement Award by the
Marquis Who's Who Publication Board. On February 9, 2019, along with

several others, I was recognized by the Hardeman County Commission for Black History as a Hardeman County History Maker and presented their North Star Award.

Plaque from National Association of State Mental Health Program Directors recognizing Evelyn Robertson for outstanding leadership as president.

I am certainly humbled by these recognitions and grateful for the acknowledgments. I am not a recognition seeker. My goal in life is to pay it forward, for I recognize that I have been tremendously blessed.

With my education and subsequent life experiences, I have become a student of history and the many lessons learned therefrom. Several years ago, I was asked to write an article for the *Masonic Voice*, the official publication of the Most Worshipful Prince Hall Grand Lodge of Tennessee. I mentioned earlier that I am a 33° Degree Prince Hall Mason. I chose to title this article, "Know Your History or Risk Being Doomed to Repeat It." I am sharing it because I think it is relevant to the present state of our society and the role, struggle, and challenges of families of color even to this day.

I began this article with a quote from Daniel Webster Davis:

> No flaming swords, no curse loud and deep,
> We bring today, though we have suffered long.

O rouse, ye race, from calm indifferent sleep,
And face life's work, —then only are we strong.

As a child and even into adulthood, I am too familiar with the Jim Crow Laws and practices commonly applied in the South. Jim Crow Laws were state and local laws imposing racial segregation enacted after the Reconstruction period in the Southern United States, that continued in force as late as 1965.

Separate but equal status for African Americans was sanctioned by laws including Supreme Court decisions such as *Plessy v. Ferguson*. During this period conditions for African Americans were consistently inferior and underfunded compared to those of white Americans. This decision institutionalized a number of economic, educational, and social disadvantages.

Jim Crow Laws mandated segregation of public schools, public places, and public transportation, and the segregation of restrooms, restaurants, and drinking fountains for whites and blacks. The military was also segregated, as were federal workplaces. The Supreme Court decision *Brown v. Board of Education* changed the educational landscape in 1954.

Black families who wanted a better life for their children during this era were faced with tremendous challenges. In spite of these laws they knew that education was the key to opening doors and ultimately forcing change. On a personal note, my grandfather, who was born into slavery in 1856, along with my grandmother raised six children. Due to the lack of educational opportunity for blacks in Hardeman County beyond the eighth grade, they had the audacity to send three of their children away from home at fifteen and sixteen years of age in the early 1920s to be boarded in order to receive a high school education. Each of them attended college; two of them earned college degrees. One of them was my father. Many families made similar sacrifices.

As a college student in 1959 and '60, at what is now Tennessee State University, I had the opportunity to participate in the dismantling of many of the discriminating practices of this era through participation in sit-ins. I marched with John Lewis, Diane Nash, Curtis Murphy, and hundreds of other college students in Nashville. This experience played a pivotal role in charting the course of my life. Much of my inspiration came from my family and the Master Masons in my community.

Many prominent Prince Hall Masons have contributed to the success and progress of our race and the success of this nation. To name a few, I would include Bro. Thurgood Marshall, Bro. Phillip A. Randolph, Bro. Benjamin Mays, Bro. W.E.B. DuBois, Bro. Andrew Young, Bro. Benjamin Hooks, Bro. Arthur A. Schomburg, Bro. Absalom Jones, Bro. John H. Johnson, Bro. Medgar Evers, Bro. Edward Kennedy "Duke" Ellington, Bro. Alex Haley, Bro. Maynard Jackson, Bro. W. C. Handy, Bro. Ossie Davis, Bro. Booker T. Washington, and Bro. Daniel Hale Williams. Obviously, many others could be a part of this list.

As we fast-forward to the present, we can now boast of having an African American president of the United States, numerous black congressional representatives, and two black US Senators. As significant as these accomplishments are, we are still faced with numerous socioeconomic challenges. We may not have the Ku Klux Klan killing us now, but we are killing ourselves. Black-on-black crime is rampant, unemployment is disproportionate, educational attainment is still low, and widespread poverty in 2015 is unacceptable but is a reality. The incarceration rate of African Americans is so high that young black men without a high school diploma are more likely to go to jail than to find a job; this causes the breakup of families and instills further poverty upon them. The incarceration rate for African Americans is about 3,074 per 100,000 residents, which is more than six times as high as the national average.

As Master Masons of past generations have stepped up to address the challenges of their times, we must do the same. The challenges that we face today are as significant as the challenges forced upon us by Jim Crow.

The conditions that created challenges in Sanford, Florida; Ferguson, Missouri; Baltimore; and New York City in recent times are symptoms of the ills that we as African Americans are faced with. Unfortunately, distrust of law enforcement and overreaction by law enforcement draw national attention. I submit that poverty, single-parent households, unemployment, lack of education, and hopelessness are huge contributors to these unfortunate incidents. The emotional toll of these incidents impacts not only families directly but the nation as a whole. Race is a topic of relevance long after the Jim Crow laws have been stricken from the books. Change has to come from the heart and not just from legislation.

As Master Masons, what is our responsibility? I think first we must lead by example. We can't just talk the talk; we must walk the walk. We must be strong advocates for justice, fairness, and opportunity. We must be visible in our communities as advocates, seeking dialogue and communication with those who may have a contrarian view. We must convey that we are all God's children, and not only do black lives matter—all lives matter. God loves all his children. Seeking opportunities to be visible at churches, Boys and Girls Clubs, schools, and after-school activities, are all ways that we can make a difference. We can also make a difference by being mentors. Many organizations are seeking men of color to get involved. We must also be active in the political process, seeking out and electing individuals who share our sense of compassion and fairness. We must hold these individuals accountable.

My brothers, claiming our communities and saving this generation should be our priority. Business as usual is not sufficient. What a great opportunity for us as Prince Hall Masons to be leaders that the present times call for. God Bless.[6]

---

[6] *The Tennessee Masonic Voice*, the official publication of the Most Worshipful Grand Lodge of Tennessee, Spring/Summer Issue 2015, pages 1, 5, 7–8, 12.

Son Jeffrey at Tennessee State University receiving B.S. Degree, 1987.

Daughter Sheila receiving Doctor of Science Degree
from Rocky Mountain University.

Grand Son Malik receiving B.S. Degree in 2019
from Middle Tennessee State University.

Grand Daughter Jasmine receiving B. S. Degree
from Middle TN State University, 2020.

Aunt Myrtle L. Robertson, B.S. Degree Home
Economics from Tennessee State University.

Cornerstone HCTS, later named Allen-White High
School, Crawford Robertson listed as Treasurer.

Father Evelyn Robertson Sr., B. S. Degree in
Agriculture Tennessee State University.

Robertson Journal

Robertson Journal

IX

Robertson Farm Legacy

According to the 2012 US Census of Agriculture, African Americans own less than 1 percent of all farms across the country. Many factors contribute to the loss of African American farms. Issues related to cost of operation, the dynamics of technology, globalization, aging workforce, and a less-than-even playing field regarding lending policies are all factors. Currently, there are less than 18,000 black farmers in the United States, and they till fewer than three million acres. In the 1990s the average black farmer was cultivating less than 120 acres of land, and half of those were attempting to survive on fifty acres or less. Black farmers in the US, to put it bluntly, have had a tremendous challenge to own land and to operate independently.

The Crawford Robertson family has been tremendously blessed to maintain ownership of its land acquired in 1888, 1896, and 1904, totaling 187 acres, for now 134 years. The reader should not assume that this has been achieved without difficulty and challenges. There have been many obstacles over this almost century and a half, among them the economic national ups and downs, the Great Depression, recessions, the boll weevil epidemics, other crop infestations, climate and weather adversities, and certainly fund availability to procure, plant, and harvest. Certain ill-advised business decisions have also played into this scenario as well. I am reminded here of the gospel song by R. C. Ward, "Think of His Goodness to You":

> When waves of affliction sweep over the soul,
> And sunlight is hidden from view,

If ever you're tempted to fret or complain,
Just think of His goodness to you.

The world may forsake you, and those whom you trust
May prove to be false and untrue;
There's one you can trust even unto the end;
Just think of His goodness to you.

Misfortune's dark cloud may hang over the way,
Despite your best efforts to do;
The Savior is guarding your treasure up there;
Just think of His goodness to you.

When dear ones are taken away from you here,
You loved with affection so true,
Look unto the Savior for strength to endure,
And think of His goodness to you.

These words from R. C. Ward appropriately describe the presence of God with the Robertson family that has endured to this day.

Middle Tennessee State University in Murfreesboro has a Center for Historic Preservation (CHP). It has many functions, one of those functions is to recognize and award designation of Century Farms. Through the CHP the Robertson farm was awarded designation as a Century Farm on November 1, 2004. A Century Farm is a farm that has been in the same family for a minimum of a hundred years and been continuously operational during that period of time. Deeds, financial tranactiions and other farm operational documents are required to support this designation. In 2004 it was rare for an African American farm in Tennessee to have this designation. I believe the Robertson farm was the second African-American farm to be so designated in Tennessee.

The Robertson family farm was entered on the National Register of Historic Places by the United States Department of Interior on November 8, 2007. This designation was from a recommendation of the Tennessee State Historic Commission.

The Robertson Farm has come full circle from an operational status.

Early in its history it was the patriarch Crawford and his sons operating the farm. This endured to the early 1960s, when Johnny, Crawford's second eldest son, was the last official descendant to operate the farm. From the mid-sixties to the early 2000s A. J. Robertson, a cousin, was the principal operator of the farm. He had purchased a portion of the land owned by Johnny which he farmed, and he leased other land owned by other family members for many years.

A.J. and my aunt Myrtle co-owned twenty-five to thirty head of cattle during her lifetime. A.J. had a large hog and goat operation for many years. Due to financial issues, A.J. sold his interest in seventy acres to the author in 1986 but continued to lease or rent acreage and operate his beef cattle operation until his failing health forced him to retire from farming. He resided in the home that was built in the early 1930s as a tenant or sharecroppers' home. He was promised that home for the duration of his life. He expired in 2016.

Following A.J.'s departure as principal operator, the operations required a different approach. There was no Crawford Robertson heir interested or available to operate the farm. Even though I resided on the farm in a residence that I built in 1964 and solely owned, I had no desire at this stage of my life to engage in day-to-day farm operation. As referenced earlier, my career had ventured into other avenues: education, behavioral health administration, and economic and community development. My son and daughter chose other vocational paths and do not live in the area. Factors associated with this decision involved the availability of workforce, the cost of equipment and machinery, the advent of technology, funding, etc.

With these apparent factors the decision was made to lease/rent the land. On a per acre rent basis the land is rented to one of the larger farm operators in the area. A total of 110 acres of the 187 acres is rented. The cultivated land produces cotton, corn, and soybeans. The rest of the land is comprised of a pasture area with a pond; timber and the other acreage surrounds the two residences on the farm. I might point out that one of the most significant changes in land cultivation in contrast to the era of Crawford Robertson is the use of the no-till approach to farming today. This approach saves the soil and minimizes erosion.

Future development will include development of a recreational lake and exploring ways to promote agritourism. The family continues to possess a wide assortment of antiques and farm implements that are a throwback to a long-gone era of farm operation. This includes household items as well as farm implements.

Continuity of family ownership of the Robertson farm is a priority, and trust arrangements have been pursued to assure this continuity of the Robertson farm legacy.

I am grateful to have been in a position to assure the preservation of the farm and its heritage. Though I am not actively engaged in farming, I tremendously enjoy the rural life and seeing on an annual basis the fruits that this land produces. To God be the glory.

Hugholene in Cotton Field on Farm,

Harvest Scene in Robertson yard, 2015,

Pear from 100 year old pear tree on farm

Dinner Bell on farm,

Gate showing one of entrances to Robertson farm,

Tenant House on farm.

Epilogue

As referenced in chapter I, I have been amazed at the relationships that my family has had with some of the historic figures and institutions of Hardeman County. For example, W. E. Farley, a prominent businessman and merchant from Whiteville, Tennessee, sold the initial farm land to Crawford (75 acres) that ultimately became the initial acquisition of the Robertson family.

Isaac Kahn was one of the Founders of the Bank of Bolivar (now CB&S). I served there as a director for ten years beginning in the 1980s. Mr. Kahn sold my grandfather 100.5 acres of land in 1904. The Kahn house is one of the historic homes in Bolivar, Tennessee, and is often featured as a visitors and tourist attraction. The house was built circa 1877.

Dr. Edwin Cocke, psychiatrist and native of Whiteville, Tennessee, served as superintendent of Western Mental Health Institute from 1918 to 1936. He served in a dual capacity as commissioner of the Department of Institutions and Superintendent at Western. I also served as superintendent at Western and commissioner of the Tennessee Department of Mental Health and Mental Retardation. Due to age and timing our paths never crossed. We also had something else in common in that he was also an author.

Crawford Robertson was instrumental in the founding of Allen-White School. He served as trustee and treasurer. His daughter, Myrtle, worked there for forty years; I worked there from 1962 to 1970, and my mother, Pearl, served as cafeteria manager at Allen-White for twenty years.

In the county history Elcanaan Baptist Church in Whiteville is referred to. This is the church where my family has worshipped for many years. My Uncle Vivian served as a clerk there. My aunt Myrtle served as clerk, and my wife, Hugholene, performs those duties today. I serve there as chairman of the board of deacons.

The Hardeman County Court (Commission) is mentioned prominently in the county's history. I had the honor of serving thirteen years on the commission representing the Whiteville area. During those election cycles, I never had an opponent.

In a small community (or county) it is obviously easy to have contacts with people doing positive things. As with my family, some may have been direct and some indirect. The Robertson's have had these opportunities going back many generations and have used them to their advantage.

As I conclude this family journey to date, I am optimistic and hopeful that more positive history is to be made by Robertson's going forward. I am frequently reminded of the poem "Invictus" by William Ernest Henley, which I recited as a youth and has been a significant presence with me throughout my life. The poem reads as follows:

> Out of the night that covers me,
>   Black as the pit from pole to pole,
> I thank whatever gods may be
>   For my unconquerable soul.
> In the fell clutch of circumstance
>   I have not winced nor cried aloud.
> Under the bludgeoning of chance
>   My head is bloody, but unbowed.
> Beyond this place of wrath and tears
>   Looms but the Horror of the shade,
> And yet the menace of the years
>   Finds and shall find me unafraid.
> It matters not how strait the gate,
>   How charged with punishments the scroll,
> I am the master of my fate,
>   I am the captain of my soul.

Robertson's have certainly faced adversity as Henley's poem relates, but have demonstrated a human spirit and an ability to overcome in dark and trying times. Faith in God, hard work, endurance, and perseverance have been constants with this family and certainly are the necessary ingredients going forward.

Speaking of going forward, unfortunately many of the conditions and circumstances that the Robertson family and other families similarly situated had to endure persist, and those old attitudes continue to exist in our society today. The cultural and racial chasm is still very prevalent. The civil rights movement did not eradicate racism, nor did the election of an African American president catapult us into a post-racial nation.

The laws of the land and the legislation referenced in this book have been important in changing some of our cultural relationships from a legal standpoint, but having a change of heart and willingness to accept each other as brothers and sisters is the real answer to this problem. Race has plagued our nation for four hundred years. Without the change of heart, it is conceivable that the issue will be in our midst for the foreseeable future, making it more challenging for this nation to realize the dream of our founders of liberty and justice for all. May we strive to continue to meet that mandate.

Appendix

Generation Chart

Evelyn C. Robertson, Jr.

b - 11/19/1941
Pb - Winchester, TN
M - 10/13/1963

Evelyn C. Robertson, Sr.

b - 1910
Pb - Whiteville, TN
M - 03/25/1937
d - 07/16/1955
Pd - Whiteville, TN

Crawford Robertson

b - 04/04/1856
Pb - Arkansas
M - 09/12/1892
d - 12/17/1937
Pd - Whiteville, TN

Henry Neely

b - 1825
Pb - Virginia (Gotencourt)
M -
d - 1910
Pd -

Cornelia Robertson

b - 1833
Pb - Virginia
M -
d - 01/28/1908
Pd -

Matthew Robertson

Mary Robertson

Cora P. Robertson

b - 09/12/1870
Pb - Fayette County (Oakland, TN)
M - 09/12/1892
d - 1950
Pd - Whiteville, TN

Andy Pierce

b - 1853
Pb - Fayette County
M -
d - 1929
Pd - Fayette County

Ann Pierce

b - 1855
Pb - Fayette County
M -
d -
Pd - Fayette County

Pearl B. Robertson

b - 05/07/1912
Pb - Bolivar, TN
M - 03/25/1937
d - 04/13/1999

Nathaniel (Nat) Brewer

b - 1870
Pb - Bolivar, TN
M - 12/17/1896
d - 1957
Pd - Bolivar, TN

Charles Brewer

b - 02/08/1829
Pb -
M -
d - 10/20/1910
Pd -

Elizabeth Brewer

b - 1834
Pb -
M -
d -
Pd -

Mattie R. Brewer

b - 1876
Pb - Bolivar, TN
M - 12/17/1896
d -
Pd - Bolivar, TN

Key:
b - Date of Birth
Pb - Place of Birth
M - Date of Marriage
d - Date of Death
Pd - Place of Death

Descendants Chart

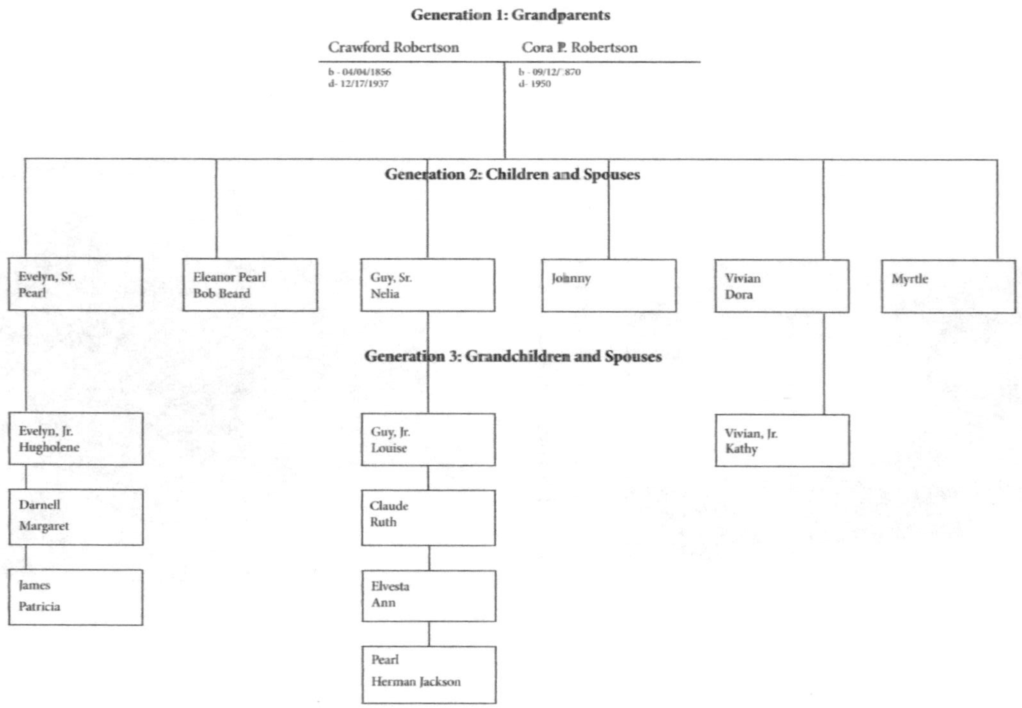

Generation 1: Grandparents

Crawford Robertson
b - 04/04/1856
d - 12/17/1937

Cora P. Robertson
b - 09/12/1870
d - 1950

Generation 2: Children and Spouses

- Evelyn, Sr. / Pearl
- Eleanor Pearl / Bob Beard
- Guy, Sr. / Nelia
- Johnny
- Vivian / Dora
- Myrtle

Generation 3: Grandchildren and Spouses

- Evelyn, Jr. / Hugholene
- Darnell / Margaret
- James / Patricia
- Guy, Jr. / Louise
- Claude / Ruth
- Elvesta / Ann
- Pearl / Herman Jackson
- Vivian, Jr. / Kathy

Photos – Family Gatherings, events, milestones and celebrations

Paternal Grand Parents, Grand Father Crawford,
Grand Mother Cora, and Aunt Myrtle

Father, Evelyn Sr.,

Mother Pearl,

Aunt Maggie,

Robertson Farm Residence,

Uncles Vivian and Johnny in Johnny's Model T,

Aunt Myrtle and Uncle Vivian,

Aunt Elnora,

Evelyn Sr. with horse,

Brothers Darnell, Evelyn & James,

Hugholene with daughter Sheila.

Maternal Grand Parents, Grand Mother Mattie,
Cousin Theresa and Grand Father Nat.

My grandfather, Nat Brewer was the father of twelve (12) children from two marriages. Their names include Arthur, George, Andrew, Mary, Isabell, Tommie, Sammy, Mamie, Lewis, Maggie, Pearl, and Mattie.

Many of Nat's children sought to avoid farm life in the South and the limits of citizenship afforded to African Americans during Reconstruction and the Jim Crow era. They became a part of the great migration and headed north, many of them landing in Chicago and other parts of Illinois. Jobs and other accommodations were more abundant there, even though second-class citizenship was still evident due to the color of their skin. Despite this, many fared well and reached back to other siblings who joined them in the environment of the north.

My uncle Arthur was a horse trainer in Chicago and worked in this industry many years. His place of employment was the Robin Hood Ranch in Hinsdale, Illinois. My uncle Sammy was a steel mill worker in Chicago. My aunt Mattie was an educator in the school system in Hardeman County, Tennessee. She matriculated at Lane College in Jackson, Tennessee. My first cousin Lila and her husband Fred Teer were educators and activists in East St. Louis, Illinois. Their daughter Barbara was a writer, producer, teacher, actress and visionary and in 1968 founded Harlem's National Black Theatre (NBT). This theatre is still active and is in Harlem at 2031 Fifth Avenue in New York City. She was formerly married to Godfrey Cambridge, the actor and entertainer. Her sister Frederica was a Congress of Racial Equality (CORE) field secretary. She worked closely with Eldridge Cleaver and Stokely Carmichael in the civil rights struggle of the '60s. Other known Brewer descendants have had successful careers in education, law, and the medical field. The author currently owns the home that his grandparents owned in Bolivar, Tennessee. They were among the first African Americans to own a home in this area of Market Street, which is east of the town.

I am very proud of my Brewer heritage.

Steven receiving degree from Tennessee State University,
pictured his father Darnell & Uncle Evelyn,

Family at Kent State University where daughter
Sheila received Masters Degree,1991.

Family gathering.

Myrtle, Ann & Pearl

Fourth of July
celebration with cousins.

Evelyn & Hugholene at event

Pearl, Hugholene & Evelyn

Evelyn at event

Classmates-Class of 1959

Evelyn receiving award

Son Jeffrey

Lafayette & Family

Darnell with Children

Evelyn & Hugholene with Jasmine at graduation

Myrtle & Nephews, Elvesta, Claude & Guy

My '51 Plymouth across from Farm House

Evelyn & Hugholene's wedding portrait, 1963.

Myrtle, Pearl, Pat & Sheila

 Your AncestryDNA Results reveal your unique story —
who your ancestors were and where they came from.

Results as of:
18 Nov 2019

DNA Results Summary for Evelyn Robertson

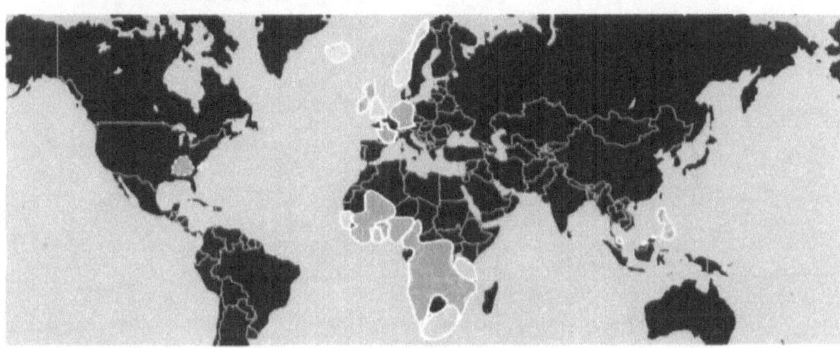

Ethnicity Estimate

England, Wales & Northwestern Europe	29%
Nigeria	23%
Cameroon, Congo & Southern Bantu Peoples	18%
Mali	11%
Benin & Togo	6%
Ireland & Scotland	3%
Ghana	2%
Senegal	2%
France	2%
Norway	1%
Southern & Eastern Africa Hunter-Gatherers	1%
Germanic Europe	1%
Philippines	1%

Additional Communities

Early North Carolina African Americans

Kentucky, Tennessee, Georgia, Alabama & Mississippi African Americans

DNA Results for Evelyn C. Robertson Jr.,

Robertson Service Honored

Evelyn Robertson Jr. was presented with an Award of Excellence in Community Support at the Tennessee Primary Care Association's Annual Leadership Conference held in Franklin. The award recognizes community members for their support of Community Health Center programs through their participation on a Community Health Center Board, as policy makers, or in the community.

Robertson was nominated by the Hardeman County Community Health Center (HCCHC). Mary Heinzen, CEO, said the nomination of Mr. Robertson Jr. was for many reasons.

"Mr. Evelyn Roberson, Jr. has been a board member for Hardeman County Community Health Center since 1996. He has served as chair, vice-chair and in other board leadership roles for many of those years. He has been instrumental in the growth of our clinics and services over the years. Though is he now retired from paid work, Mr. Robertson is very active in many community boards, both locally and on a West Tennessee regional basis. He is a former Commissioner of the Department of Mental Health, former Superintendent of Western Mental Health Institute, and former director of the Southwest Tennessee Development District. He has served on boards and councils related to community health, mental health, education, and numerous other projects. He brings considerable management expertise to our board, and the communities he lives in and near. He has been at the forefront in our Corporation's efforts for succession planning, strategic planning, and behavioral health integration.

"During the past year, he has been a tireless and vocal advocate for the need for the State of Tennessee to expand Medicaid coverage. His knowledge, expertise, leadership and vision, have enabled HCCHC managers and board members to remain strong and progressive in their efforts to expand access to primary health care and to improve the overall lives of the people who live in West Tennessee. He is greatly admired and appreciated for his professional and focused dedication as a community servant and leader."

Photo: Mary Heinzen, Robertson, Kathy Wood-Dobbins the CEO of TPCA, and Lisa Terry the TPCA Board President.

Robertson Service Honored Article

The Center for Historic Preservation
Research and Public Service since 1984
P.O. Box 80
Middle Tennessee State University
Murfreesboro, Tennessee 37132
Office: (615) 898-2947 • Fax: (615) 898-5614
http://histpres.mtsu.edu/histpres/

November 2, 2004

Mr. Evelyn C. Robertson, Jr.
2665 Newsom Rd.
Whiteville, TN 38075

Dear Mr. Robertson:

Congratulations and welcome to the Tennessee Century Farms program! We have read and reviewed the application for the Robertson Farm and we are pleased to add it to our state wide documentary record of family farms in Tennessee. You have provided a well-documented account of your family farm which is certainly a landmark property in Hardeman County.

To welcome your family to the program, you will find enclosed an official certificate of recognition, suitable for framing. To learn more about the Tennessee Century Farms, you or others in your family may want to visit our electronic web page at www.mtsu.edu/~histpres. You will find the Century Farms program under "Center Initiatives." A listing of certified Century Farms by county is included and we will be adding your farm in the next few days. We will also send a news release to your local newspaper to recognize your Century Farm status.

The Tennessee Department of Agriculture (TDOA) established the Century Farm program in 1975 and county historians and county farm agents continue to help locate and certify farm families who would like to be a part of the program. Over 1000 family farms, representing every county in the state, are currently designated as certified Century Farms. We are very pleased to announce that the TDOA has resumed its program that offers a free metal sign to each Century Farm. Please find enclosed a newsletter announcing that and providing other information about the program. I will inform the TDOA that you are eligible to receive a sign and they will be in touch in the near future telling you how to receive your sign. If you have questions, do not hesitate to call me.

Thank you again for your interest in the Century Farm program and for your application. We consider each of the family farms in this program to be a "Tennessee treasure."

Sincere regards,

Caneta Skelley Hankins
Director, Tennessee Century Farms Program

Letter from the Center for Historic Preservation

www.ingramcontent.com/pod-product-compliance
Lightning Source LLC
Chambersburg PA
CBHW031137250726
48655CB00002B/715